Kids Can Think

Kids Can Think

Philosophical Challenges for the Classroom

Ron Gilmore

ROWMAN & LITTLEFIELD
Lanham • Boulder • New York • London

Published by Rowman & Littlefield
A wholly owned subsidiary of The Rowman & Littlefield Publishing Group, Inc.
4501 Forbes Boulevard, Suite 200, Lanham, Maryland 20706
www.rowman.com

Unit A, Whitacre Mews, 26-34 Stannary Street, London SE11 4AB

Copyright © 2016 by Ron Gilmore

All rights reserved. No part of this book may be reproduced in any form or by any electronic or mechanical means, including information storage and retrieval systems, without written permission from the publisher, except by a reviewer who may quote passages in a review.

British Library Cataloguing in Publication Information Available

Library of Congress Cataloging-in-Publication Data

Names: Gilmore, Ron, 1966- author.
Title: Kids can think : philosophical challenges for the classroom / Ron Gilmore.
Description: Lanham : Rowman & Littlefield Publishing Group, Inc., [2016]
Identifiers: LCCN 2016031044 (print) | LCCN 2016031129 (ebook) |
 ISBN 9781475829518 (cloth : alk. paper) | ISBN 9781475829525 (pbk. : alk. paper) |
 ISBN 9781475829532 (Electronic)
Subjects: LCSH: Philosophy—Study and teaching.
Classification: LCC B52 .G49 2016 (print) | LCC B52 (ebook) | DDC 372.8—dc23
 LC record available at https://lccn.loc.gov/2016031044

∞™ The paper used in this publication meets the minimum requirements of American National Standard for Information Sciences—Permanence of Paper for Printed Library Materials, ANSI/NISO Z39.48-1992.

Printed in the United States of America

Contents

Preface		vii
PART I: The Culture of Philosophical Thinking in Schools		**1**
1	Using the Book	3
2	Patterns of Thinking for Philosophy	7
3	Classroom Culture: No Right, No Wrong	11
PART II: Scenarios for the Classroom		**17**
4	Do We Live in a Colorful World?	19
5	Do You Believe What You See?	25
6	No Future	31
7	A Red Sock?	35
8	The Present	39
9	The Me Gene	43
10	The Infinite Line	47
11	Who Is I?	51
12	What Is an Object?	55
13	Who Are You?	59
14	Not Fair	63

15	Can Altruism Be Genuine?	69
16	Present Again	73
17	Know What You're Thinking?	77
18	Is Choice a Good Thing?	83
19	Is Anything Random?	87
20	The Bare Substratum	93
21	Infinite Universes	97
22	Infinity	101
23	Silence	105
24	Disliking Liking	109
25	The Search for Life	113
26	Confusion	119
27	Waking Dreams	125
About the Author		129

Preface

Philosophy conjures up images of ancient men in beards and cloaks or elderly greying professors tucked up in some disorganized study at the top of a university tower, and for too long education systems have bowed to the needs of science, technology, and commerce and have slowly pushed it into the realms of the quaint, academic and irrelevant.

Pupils today have the potential to reap the benefits the digital revolution is bringing but if educators are not careful we will be guilty of doing nothing more than exposing children to vast, unmanageable quantities of information, and the mind, untrained to be discerning and cautious will be unable to distinguish and utilize quality information from the inaccurate, the misleading, or the invented. The ceaseless flow of information becomes the detritus that blocks the flow of the river and the digital age becomes our hindrance.

A current Google search for *global warming* throws up some 57,600,000 results, and a more specific search for *global warming rainforest Brazil* will find a pupil confronted with just under half a million hits. Many of these are likely to contain erroneous information presented as being factual whilst others have opinionated, political slants.

Sites that are so-called child friendly are frequently inaccurate and fail to provide balanced views. They are constructed by well-meaning amateurs and often result in links to other sites of similar dubious quality, often with some form of game attached. If educated adults find it difficult to negotiate their way through this our children stand little chance unless we train them to be skeptical, critical thinkers.

The modern world is often guilty of shying away from ethics. Technology is brought into the classroom as well as almost every facet of our lives, all in the name of progress. I often ask my colleagues the question, "Where is this *progress* leading us to?" and I am met with a stony silence. This is a probing and awkward question. Many turn their back on it or perceive it to be shrouded in negativity but if we are to educate our pupils with ethical savvy we must train them in the art of philosophical skepticism. This is the antithesis of negativity and lies at the heart of informed decision making.

Philosophical training is about establishing doubts without helplessness. Without philosophy, there are no doubts but helplessness in abundance. With the incredible scope of possibility that our children are growing up with, good decision making is perhaps more important than it has ever been.

Slowly the world, whether it be in commercial, political, or social spheres, is becoming aware of the power of the mind trained in philosophy. Philosophers are sought after once again. Businesses and governments wrestle with the same complex ideas that have plagued for centuries. They provide the ring and the players but it is the philosopher who provides the techniques that drive success.

Most curricula have a narrow scope for philosophical thinking. Even the more progressive curricula that promote understanding on the basis of pupil investigation and exploration have limitations because they always demand assessable outcomes. There is a preoccupation with teachers having to provide evidence. At the end of any inquiry there must be a piece of writing, a poster, a play, a model, or some other tangible piece of evidence.

Such outcomes are often evidence of the pupil's ability to conform to the expectations of the curriculum. It may keep education authorities and parents impressed but the type of thinking that is required in the production of such evidence often lacks a skeptical depth. It is easy to find out and regurgitate in a form that pleases but research is not merely about finding out but questioning. It is about taking thinking out of the proverbial box and this can be uncomfortable for educationalists who have predetermined standards and expectations and steer pupils into conformity.

Imagine a class which has been working on a unit investigation of environmental issues. The pupil who produces an assessment leaflet promoting recycling and renewable energy will be deemed a success. The pupil who produces a leaflet dismissing renewables as being political propaganda risks negative feedback.

In philosophy there is no right or wrong outcome; instead, the emphasis is on the quality of the thinking and reasoning.

A sense of conformity will most likely always lie at the heart of education. Standards have to be met and society demands a strong element of control. There may be no escaping this but there must be a place in the curriculum for a time when pupils can be liberated from target setting and the production of proof. The real evidence is in the thinking that works in the brain.

For a session a week, philosophy can be celebrated for what it is without having to be transferred into some evidential form. This is liberating for pupils but for teachers too. Too often they are so preoccupied with recording progress on rubrics that the simple wonder of children's ability to think creatively is lost.

It is time to reintroduce philosophy to our pupils and make it a central tenet of their education as it will give them the tools with which to navigate the trillions (and rapidly growing) number of pages of information available to them at the click of a mouse. It will enable them to become the discerning decision makers of the future.

This book is not about bringing Plato or Descartes into the classroom. There may be a legitimate place for introducing children to formal philosophy but the aim of this book is about nurturing patterns of thinking, inspiring questioning minds and intellectual reasoning. Above all, it is about having fun with thinking.

Part I

THE CULTURE OF PHILOSOPHICAL THINKING IN SCHOOLS

Chapter 1

Using the Book

The ideas in the chapters that follow (scenarios in the book) can be used for children as young as 9 up to 90 and beyond.

Each chapter invites the pupils to consider perplexing questions that are easy to relate to. The aim is not for them to draw conclusions but to explore ideas in free and imaginative ways.

Younger children are often capable of complex thinking and are often more open and uninhibited with their insights than older pupils. The young have not been trained in the art of conformity and may go off on wild tangents. This is the mind's natural way of exploring thinking and so-called *off-task* thinking is often the richest both for pupils and teacher. Traditionally, teachers are experts in the art of keeping pupils on task and it takes conscious decision making to allow pupils to explore their own thinking. It may appear random to the educator used to neatly packaged learning strategies but thinking is never random.

Allowing the pupils freedom in thinking will almost instantly trigger spontaneous and creative thinking. The teacher's role is to join in this process and to respond to pupils in a way that leads them to making use of the basic philosophical thinking tools.

Consider these examples:

Pupil: *If he does that to her then that makes her do something to someone else who does something to someone else and it goes on and on.*

Teacher: *Yes, it's kind of like the weather. One movement of air causes other movements. It has a knock on effect.*

This response encourages the use of comparison. The teacher has modeled the form of thinking. Asking the pupil for their own comparison can make them feel put on the spot and may hamper their flow of thought.

Children are natural imitators and will subconsciously respond to the teacher's modeling and they will, in time, incorporate the strategies into their own thinking.

Furthermore, by the teacher responding in this way, the message to the pupil is *I am interested in what you have to say*. Responses such as *Oh, that's interesting. What do you think?* and *I see. That's a great point* are vague and don't actually show the pupil that there has been real engagement in their thinking on the teacher's part. This is not to criticize the teacher—often there is not the time or opportunity to fully engage with the pupils, which makes a lesson or perhaps more accurately, a discussion of a philosophical nature, so valuable.

It is an opportunity for pupils to gain self-esteem on the basis purely of their thinking, not as is usually the case, on a physical outcome.

The scenarios should be seen as being a stimulus for thinking conceptually. It is the thinking patterns and their complexity that is important rather than any outcomes, and as such they are not in any way prescriptive. The intention is the very opposite—they aim to open the mind to all sorts of possibilities rather than channel thinking down specific paths as is so often the case in the classroom.

The teacher may choose to read an introductory scenario to the class as a whole or pupils may be asked to read it in preparation for the lesson depending on the age level and reading ability of the pupils.

After reading, a short open discussion can be held. This sets the mood and should be allowed to go in any direction. Allowing pupils to stray not only gives the teacher an insight into their train of thought; it also permits the pupil to explore connections that are apparent to them. Often, the richest thinking comes from lines of thought which are surprising and unpredictable. Again, it should be stressed that the goal of the teacher is to direct a style of philosophical thinking, i.e. addition/deletion, analysis/synthesis, comparison/contrast, not to dictate the content of the thinking.

Many of the chapters have questions contained within them. These can be read within the context of the whole chapter or the teacher may wish to focus on a question and allow discussion to run from it. The teacher needs to constantly gauge the interest of the pupils at any given point and capitalize on that interest. There is nothing to be gained by striving to complete a chapter if it means skipping opportunities where pupils naturally find they want to engage.

It is important to establish a mindset where pupils appreciate thinking is something which develops. Ideas are there to stimulate and to be mulled over.

They are not there to generate outcome or a sense of completion. Indeed, many of the ideas are many centuries old and are still awaiting conclusions. The nature of philosophical thought depends on the evolution of ideas unlike science where definitive answers are sought. For many pupils this will be a new way of thinking about problems in the school environment but it makes use of the pupil's natural manner of inquiring. The excitement lies in the questions and the inquiry more than in the answers.

Each scenario is followed by a set of thinking routines which aim to bring structure to the thinking. These can be used in both whole class settings or small group settings and provide simple, open tasks which can be explored at a level appropriate to the age group. The aim is not to have an assessed outcome. If pupils have the feeling of being assessed their thinking will become restricted and they will slip into thinking in terms of being right or wrong.

The Think About It sections offer the teacher some ideas to follow up the text and discussions but again, it must be stressed that they are intended to be flexible, not prescriptive. The ideas can be adapted to be used at any point within the chapters.

The main benefit that comes from using them is that all pupils are included. In open discussions it will always be the case that some pupils are more engaged than others while others are happy to sit back and let others do the thinking. The routines require all pupils to take a role and give them the opportunity to have their thinking valued rather than judged.

That pupils feel their thinking is valued is the key concern. The great reward is in the value, not in being right or wrong. In most scenarios there is no scope for right or wrong responses. Pupils who are generally under responsive in ordinary classroom situations often find a sense of relief in this attitude. There are few greater rewards for a teacher than to see the under-responsive pupil begin to sparkle under the pleasure of free thinking.

Standalone philosophy lessons are great starting points to explore thinking but if the patterns of thought only exist in the philosophy class the greater purpose has been missed. If bringing rationality and logic to the way in which pupils think about the world and its problems is the aim, philosophical thinking skills must pervade across the curriculum and into everyday life. Encouraging pupils to utilize the core thinking skills in the classroom will instill a natural desire within them to probe and question intellectually.

Chapter 2

Patterns of Thinking for Philosophy

The aim of the scenarios that follow is to enable the teacher to develop three distinct patterns of thinking which will pervade all aspects of the pupil's thinking such that decision making become rational and logical. They encourage pupils to reflect on their own understanding of the world and generate questions which probe deeply. These patterns of thought may be present in the daily workings of a classroom but pupils and teachers are not always consciously aware of them.

Through the process of discussion with the teacher interacting and modeling thinking patterns, the fundamentals of philosophical thought can be established as a powerful tool in the modern learning environment and pupils quickly learn that, when challenged, conventionally accepted understandings of the world around them can and need to be challenged in ways which are constructive and make learning a dynamic and engaging process.

Where pupils were once receptacles to be filled with information they now become naturally skeptical and seekers of sound evidence—a prerequisite for constructive decision making. Established at a young age, these principles of thinking provide lifelong attitudes, essential to the negotiation of the modern world.

COMPARISON AND CONTRAST

The pupil is asked to compare two categories, considering elements which are similar and those which are not. This can take place at both specific and general levels. Compare solar panels and wind turbines—both produce renewable energy, both have carbon footprints in their production, both are in early stages of development but they differ in terms of where they might be best located; one uses the sun, the other the wind, and so on. On a more general level, pupils might be asked to compare politics and technology—both seek to improve standards of living, both are forward looking but politics is about ideas whereas technology builds specific tools.

The act of comparing compels the thinker to consider like and unlike elements in any given situation and results in a deep level of processing. A pupil asked to divide 12 by a ¼ can be asked to compare this question to one they know the answer to: divide 12 by 3. Through the process of comparison, the pupil can identify the similarities and apply this understanding to the first problem. Most problems do not exist in complete isolation but have similarities to known elements; being able to identify these is a crucial step in finding solutions.

Comparison and contrast form the basis of much scientific thinking and should be a key strategy used by pupils investigating in the classroom. Comparing the setup of one experiment with another and contrasting findings is the first step in genuine investigation whether this be at a basic primary or advanced level.

Comparing and contrasting is a basic tool of the philosopher and it encourages pupils to dig into thinking about essential and constituent elements of ideas.

ANALYSIS AND SYNTHESIS

Analysis and synthesis form the basis of what philosophers term the *philosophical attitude of inquiry*. In analysis, the pupil is asked to take something apart and examine individual components and consider the workings of each. They may consider the wide concept of *communication* and break it down into a range of aspects: speaking, art, emailing, social networking, etc. A classroom exploration of *water* may be broken down into drinking, sewage, water cycle, ice, etc.

Analysis on a general level is common practice in the classrooms of the twenty-first century but such wide-scoped topics often don't provide pupils with the opportunity to dig deeper and continue the process of analysis.

In exploring drinking water, pupils could consider bottled water. In one Grade 5 class pupils looked into the chemical makeup of different bottled waters compared to government regulated tap water; they considered the transportation cost, financial and environmental, of shifting millions of liters of bottled water around the country on a daily basis; and they considered the environmental impact of the plastics used to make the bottles. They thought about the jobs associated with the production and sale of bottled water.

Previous classes hadn't analyzed in such depth and came to a simplified conclusion that it is good to drink bottled water. The class who analyzed in greater depth became intellectually cynical and deferred making any conclusions until they had more information to work with.

The process of analysis is an on-going one and conclusions are rarely definitive. It is a pragmatic practice that allows for intellectual development and promotes continual inquiry.

Many readily give their children mobile technology and the use of an increasing number of computers in our schools is celebrated but pupils sitting at computers often don't have the skills to perform any meaningful analysis. Those with a basic grounding in philosophical analysis will ask the questions most fail to ask.

By working on this process the pupil understands the complexities that lie beneath generalities. This lies at the heart of most scientific enquiry where the topics to be explored become ever narrower and more specific; thus a cancer researcher may dedicate their career to exploring the workings of one specific cell.

Synthesis is the reverse. Smaller bits of knowledge are brought together to create new possibilities. Individual studies of species in the rain forest, when brought together, give a clearer picture of environmental concerns. Thousands of small technological innovations have come together to create today's mobile devices.

Children are innately good at synthesizing in their play and instinctively bring objects and ideas together to create possibilities in the way they explore the world. The process is creative and can lead to thought processes and conclusions that deviate from teacher expectations. Teachers are often guilty of reigning children in so they can fulfill the needs of predetermined assessment tasks.

Synthesis, in the philosophy of the curriculum, is encouraged but in practice it is too often curtailed. The education system isn't sure how to handle *wacky* ideas and the subliminal message to children is *synthesize but in a fashion the teacher identifies with*.

Free standing lessons in philosophical thinking liberate the pupil from the constraints of curricular outcomes associated with assessed areas of the curriculum. Thinking routines encourage pupils to make any claims they so choose so long as they back them up with logical, rational thought. As in scientific hypotheses, the onus is on others to find means of disproving.

ADDITION AND DELETION

At the heart of prediction lie the philosophical tools of addition and deletion. They generate *what if?* questions by wondering what will happen if something is added to or removed from an idea. In the modern world, this is one of the most essential tools for the next generation and all too often it has been neglected, resulting in complex societal problems. The trend is to go with the flow of technology in the name of progress without paying due attention to *what if* questions.

Drones may be the future for delivering our parcels but *what if* the same drones are used by terrorists to deliver bombs? Genetic engineering can find solutions to terrible diseases but *what if* the technology feeds a designer baby marketplace? *What if* we discover mobile phones have a link to brain tumors?

More than ever, the next generation needs to be trained to add in the negatives and subtract the positives if good decisions are to be made. The skeptical mind is the one which takes steps with caution and will avoid the pitfalls that await.

Today's pupils are the first truly online generation and from their devices they control and manipulate their identities. Instinctively they add to and subtract from their personas to control how others perceive them but they often omit to apply addition and deletion to foresee the dangers and negative consequences of their online actions. Philosophy can give pupils the intellectual tools to predict what might be.

Together, these three essential tools provide the foundation of logical, inquiry-based thinking which aims to be the hallmark of the modern curriculum and the role of the educator is to model these process by utilizing them in their own thinking.

Chapter 3

Classroom Culture
No Right, No Wrong

Most traditional curricular areas have right and wrong answers and from a young age children seek the rewards associated with being *right*. This in itself is highly limiting since being *wrong* is the driving force behind the most effective learning.

Very young children, at the age of genuine learning through discovery, have no qualms about getting it *wrong*. If they did, would they ever learn to speak? Or walk? Those areas such as Social Studies where there may appear to be more flexibility are, in fact, often subject to predetermined teacher-acceptable responses. While pupils may be encouraged to think freely, typically their responses attempt to satisfy the teacher's preconceived ideas and are, therefore, restricted.

Setting up a culture in the classroom where there is no *right* nor *wrong* must come from the teacher since it is he/she who, in the pupil's eyes, is the manager of *rightness* and *wrongness*. Often it is the teacher who finds it hardest to let go.

In the first philosophy class it is essential to establish the tenet that the purpose of philosophy is not to be *right* or *wrong* but it is to be able to use reasoned logic to support a point of view. It is about the process of thinking not the outcome. Indeed, most of the big philosophical issues will never have a definitive answer.

The example: *Is there life after death?* is an ideal illustrative topic. There is no correct answer as a positive or negative response cannot ever be proved and there is a strong sense that *your ideas are as a valid as mine*. This makes it a great introductory topic. It can easily involve every individual and since it probes at the essence of existence it is something most will have already given thought to. Discussions always bring in multiple perspectives. Pupils who may usually be inattentive find themselves listening intensely to their peers, intellectual challenging occurs effortlessly and pupils naturally look for flaws in logic.

During this process of discussion, pupils will have the feeling that they are not actually working. To exacerbate this, the topic can be brought up in what appears to be an unplanned forum giving the pupils the notion that the discussion is somehow off task from the day's events. Ironically, the thinking mind is often more on task during so-called *off-task* scenarios. Potential is unleashed and pupils and teacher will be inspired to explore other topics.

Pupils often enjoy thinking of other questions that have no answers and quickly become more aware that human thinking is often about degrees rather than definitives. The aim for the philosophy class is to have pupils examine the logic of arguments and to approach thinking from varied directions. What pupils can do as fledgling philosophers is make a claim and use logic to support it. While it is not helpful to describe logic as being wrong it can be said to be flawed.

All boys like blue. One child likes blue therefore the child must be a boy.

In some religions people believe there is life after death. Yasmin believes there is life after death. Yasmin must, therefore, be religious.

Working through a few examples where the flaw is obvious allows students to understand that not all thinking is valid. It is not a free for all.

Good thinking is hard work. It requires deep concentration and energy but above all else it should be fun. Working out the mind is very similar to working out the body and if it is to have a lasting and sustainable impact it must be enjoyable.

Being free from testing and having to produce final assessable products creates a unique energy. The child allowed to play in open fields exercises in a very different way to the child participating in an organized sport. Both are valid and both have their role to play. Philosophy allows the child's mind to run in open fields.

THE RIGHT TO SPEAK

This may seem obvious in the modern classroom but it is not always easy to establish a culture in the classroom where voices are heard equally. Those most eager to share their thinking are not always the ones who are astute listeners and the avid listeners are not always those who feel confident to share their views. Students may be required to raise their hand before they can speak or the teacher may pick students randomly to give them the opportunity to express their thinking. There is a place for such regimes but there are dangers.

1. It is often the same students who raise their hands. They like their voice to be heard no matter what.
2. Selecting pupils at random can put an individual under stress—what if they have nothing to say? Stress is the single best way of blocking the thinking process.

A small red card and a small green card can be given to each student. If they don't wish to contribute they leave their card red but turn it to the green side if they feel they want to speak. This is less obtrusive than hands in the air and gives students control of their desire to speak. It is a useful technique at the start of a lesson when general ideas are gathered.

Ideas instigated by pupils should not be reinforced with praise relating to the perceived quality of the point being made as this perpetuates the *right/ wrong* phenomenon. Instead, points should be responded to by offering questions for others to explore or by the teacher actively engaging with the point.

Pupil: *There could be another planet somewhere with exactly the same people as us on it.*

Teacher: *Would they have the same thoughts and feelings as us? Might there be an infinite number of planets like this? What would happen if you were able to visit it?*

By opening the possibilities to the whole class the questioning is not necessarily directed at the pupil who made the initial point. This creates a comfortable environment where pupils know their thinking is not going to be challenged directly and the fear of having a *stupid* idea diminishes.

Once this classroom culture is established the less-willing talkers gain in confidence. Thinking needs to be fun and independent of emotional self consciousness which is all too often prevalent in the classroom.

INDIVIDUAL, GROUP OR CLASS

There is a place for all three and all have their merits.

Sessions can be started with a paper talk exercise. On three or four large pieces of paper write a starting statement related to the content of the lesson. For example: *Robots are Alive.*

Divide the class into three or four groups and start each at one of the sheets. Pupils must not speak but should write down their thoughts or questions. After two minutes, rotate the groups. Pupils can add further thoughts or write responses to other statements written by their peers. Continue the rotations until each group has visited each station.

This is an excellent way of getting every pupil involved in the thinking process and the resulting pieces of paper can offer many rich starting points for further discussions as well as getting pupils in the mood. Pupils are free to add their own thoughts on the topic or can comment on other's. Everyone is involved and can contribute in an unthreatening way.

This exercise only takes a few minutes and can be followed up by reading the introductory content of the chapter to the class. At the end ask for contributions or refer to the sheet from the first exercise. Contributions should be referred to as being *interesting* but not good as being *good* will serve to perpetuate the right/wrong culture and should be avoided. The role of the teacher here is to probe, question, and challenge, and often requires that the teacher thinks in a way which is outside the comfort zone of his/her principles. The teacher must also challenge his/her preconceived ideas in order to stimulate the pupils.

In a discussion on poverty, Adam, a ten-year-old, says: *We should give money to a beggar on the street.*

The teacher can respond in a variety of ways but should note which aspect of philosophical thinking is being triggered.

Teacher: *What if the beggar is actually just too lazy to work?* (addition).

Is it the best way to help all the poor? (analysis of a bigger picture).

After a discussion on a robotic cat, Daniella who is fourteen states: *It's not alive because it can't think for itself.*

Teacher: *A tree cannot think for itself. Does that mean it is not alive?* (comparison).

Is being able to think the only thing that makes something alive? (analysis/synthesis).

In what way is human thinking different from a computer's thinking? (comparison).

As pupils progress through sessions they may not be consciously aware of the styles they are using but the teacher will notice them adapting their thinking style in response to differing inputs and may wish to highlight the types of thinking as they occur.

Many of the tasks at the end of the scenarios allow for individuals to record their own responses. They should not be put under pressure to respond, however, as this leads to a thinking driven by expectations, not creativity. Creative thinking often takes time and no pupil should be expected to produce it on demand.

Working within a group allows individuals to have discussions. It is important that they have the opportunity to test their logic on others in their peer group and to work at building consensual views. Often, during this process all the individuals within the group will naturally start to develop their thinking.

THE ENVIRONMENT

Many school planners have become more enlightened and build schools with comfort in mind allowing flexible spaces for work of different sorts. In schools of a more traditional layout a few small measures can be taken in order to makes spaces more conducive to open discussion.

The philosophy scenarios in the book do not require desks and where possible pupils should not be sitting at one. Of course they are often a necessity but they are a potent symbol of teacher and institutional control and tend not to provide the ideal environment for creative thinking. Having pupils sit in a group on a carpet can be equally inhibiting. If they feel herded, with the teacher sitting gazing down, there is a feeling of collectivism which doesn't create the ideal environment for pupils to become individual thinkers.

In most schools it is possible to use spaces creatively. Simply pushing desks to the side of the room can raise the sense of anticipation and with it, philosophy becomes something exciting. Beanbags and cushions can create comfortable corners where discussions can take place. Asking pupils to set the classroom up in a way they want gives them ownership of the discussions and sets the tone for the lessons.

Philosophical discussions have long been associated with cafe culture. It might not be possible to build a replica Parisian cafe in the school but a canteen or dining hall area can create a novel and comfortable environment. Having pupils take turns baking cookies is a great way of making a unique atmosphere which is favorable to thinking.

Part II

SCENARIOS FOR THE CLASSROOM

Chapter 4

Do We Live in a Colorful World?

As a young fourteen-year-old, Arnie ventured into town for his first attempt at independent clothes shopping. Usually, he trailed behind his mother while she flicked through clothes on their hangers and examined washing instruction labels. After she'd selected a few items from the racks, he was sent off into the changing room where he'd struggle in the tiny confined space to undress and get dressed again. He would appear from behind the curtain dressed in each item and she would look him up and down, a hand would be placed on his shoulder and he was asked to turn around to give her a back view.

His mother would make a decision; based on what, he was never really able to establish. Now, he had to do the looking up and down in the mirror himself and wondered what he was actually looking for; no falling off his waist, no flapping round the ankles. "Make sure you try them on with your shoes on," his mother had instructed him.

Mindful of the fact that this was his first act of responsible shopping he avoided the jeans with the designer frayed cuts on the knee he quite liked the look of and instead chose a rather conservative pair of corduroy trousers in a dark blue. When he got home he went up to his bedroom, put them on and rather proudly presented himself and his purchase to his mother and sister in the kitchen. "They look super," his mother said, "dark green is a lovely color. I'm impressed."

Perplexed, he retorted, "They're dark blue. Not green."

"Well, I don't know what you see but that's what I call green. They're as green as green could be."

He looked at his sister and said, "They're blue, aren't they?"

"I would say they're green."

He had been tested for color blindness at his school's medical and had passed without any difficulty. He could pick out the numbers easily from among the color dotted mass the doctor had put in front of him.

He pondered the question: "Are my mom and I seeing the same thing but choose to give the color a different name or are we actually seeing something different from one another?"

Convinced his trousers were blue, he spent the rest of the day asking anyone he met for their opinion. About half were adamant they were blue, the other half equally adamant they were green. At the time, it never occurred to him to check the shop's pricing label so he was never able to establish the retailer's opinion. Perhaps the truth was they were bluish-green or greenish-blue. Or, perhaps there was no real color at all but what he saw was just a creation of his own brain.

The nature of color is a highly complex one and has been subject to much debate over the centuries. The first question to consider is: do physical objects have a color in their own right or do the colors only exist when there is a perceiver to perceive them? Is that red bicycle only red when someone looks at it or does it really possess a quality of redness? Put in a different way: Is it the object or the mind that actually possesses the color?

Turning to science for an answer isn't as helpful as might be hoped. It is known that objects are made up of smaller parts (atoms, electrons, all the way down to quarks) and these objects in themselves are not colored. Putting a lot of non-colored objects together should, logically, result in a larger non-colored object. So does this mean objects have no actual color?

Light is reflected off the surface of an object and how this happens is dependent on the microstructure of the object surface. The microstructures of the surface of a banana differ to those of a grape and hence the reflected light has different qualities. Of course, how we perceive the color is dependent on other factors such as the intensity and angle of light hitting the surface. A banana seen in bright daylight will appear a different color if seen under a halogen lamp but the structure of the surface remains constant.

A conclusion that an object itself has color requires the assumption that color is one and the same thing as its surface microstructure. But the question remains: Is it the object that possesses the color or the light or the way our brain interprets or perceives the light?

It would be neat and tidy if the perception of a particular blue in physical terms could be explained by making reference to its wavelength (wavelength type A will always result in perceiving the shade of blue type A) but different wavelengths of light can result in perceiving exactly the same color therefore making it impossible to define the color we perceive by its wavelength. (Wavelength A = perception A but wavelength B = perception A.)

If color doesn't have definable physical attributes perhaps it is necessary to rely on defining it in terms of perception or subjective experience. That is, it only exists because it is perceived. Such things, if they are things at all in the measurable sense, are known as qualia.

In this regard it is similar to pain which doesn't have measurable characteristics and exists as a perception making the common remark, "the pain is all in your mind," a true statement. Just as an object cannot have pleasure or pain so it cannot have color either. Remove the perceiver and the world is completely colorless.

Do we all perceive color in the same way?

The only way humans have to express their private experiences is through public language. One person may look at grass and say it is green and another will also say it is green but both are doing this because from a young age they have learned that the experience of looking at grass has the label green attached to it. The same label is used but this not to say both people actually have the same experience.

One person can try to tell another what he sees when he calls something green but he cannot give the other the experience he has. Experiences are locked into the individual and can never be shared. Humans live in a social world but their experiences must remain totally private.

David Grimshaw, now a grown adult, has been totally blind since birth. He has never experienced color in the environment. His friends have spent many hours trying to explain their experience of red to him but their explanations simply make no sense to him and the concept of redness remains as mysterious as ever. This is difficult for the sighted person to understand but when it is considered that the visible light spectrum humans can perceive is only a tiny fraction of the wavelengths of light that exist, it follows that there is much out there that is unknown.

Asking David to understand redness is similar to asking a person to imagine a color they have never seen. Imagining a totally new color isn't possible. The brain doesn't have the capacity to do this just as David's doesn't have the capacity to experience redness.

A demonstration of the importance of perception can be done very simply. Take a sheet of white paper outside, then take the same sheet inside. Most would call the paper white irrespective of its location. A photograph of the white sheet taken in both locations and digitally examined reveals that the pixel colors vary depending on the location and, interestingly, neither are actually white. It would appear perception and language dominate the experience.

In the story, the boy's mother and sister used a different language label to describe his trousers but they may or may not have perceived the same as the boy. It is just not possible to know and science can't help. The qualia are strictly private.

Yet another way of looking at the issue of color is to claim that it doesn't actually exist. There is a visual experience of the world where light is transmitted through the eyes to the brain and it is here that the coloring occurs. It is like having a black and white coloring book and the brain has a selection of colors and sets to work at coloring all visual experiences. Perhaps the boy's trousers were, after all, colorless.

Think About It

STEP 1: QUESTION
If somebody said, "I like your blue trousers," what questions might you ask them?

STEP 2: RESPONSE
Share your questions with a partner and ask them to write down their responses.

STEP 3: WONDER
What do you wonder now that you didn't wonder before?

Chapter 5

Do You Believe What You See?

Many years ago, when Aisha was a child of ten there was spate of burglaries in her neighborhood. One particular day in the summer she was sitting up in her tree-house enjoying some shady peace when she witnessed two men climbing up the drainpipe of her neighbors' house and entering a bedroom window which had been left open.

One might have expected that she would have slipped off her tree perch and alerted her newspaper-reading parents in the garden or shouted, "robbers," at the top of her voice. She did neither but found herself transfixed by what she was witnessing. Such things were to be found on Saturday night television dramas, but to have two live burglars carry out this seemingly daring act filled her with a sense of great excitement.

Later that day, two policemen arrived at their door and explained that their neighbors had suffered a burglary and they asked her parents if they had seen anything untoward. They said they hadn't and the policemen thanked them for their time, asked them to be vigilant and went to leave when all of a sudden Aisha piped up with, "I think I saw something."

She gave them what she thought was an accurate description of the two men who were dressed in jeans and wore leather jackets and she explained how they'd left the scene in a red Ford car.

It transpired that the criminals had moved to burgle another house in the area but had disturbed a large Alsatian dog which took a chunk of flesh from one of the burglar's behinds. News spread of how a man and a woman, neither of whom were wearing leather jackets, had been caught while trying to make an escape in a red van.

Aisha's powers of description, whilst being well intentioned, had in the end been short of helpful. Years later as she reflected on the incident she wondered how she could have seen all that went on so clearly yet her recall was so distorted. So was she right to believe what she saw?

The convenient answer would be a simple *yes* since most people construct what they believe to be true about the world on the basis of what they see and the impact of that not being true would be of such enormity that most people have never given the question any thought. Perhaps they fear what their thinking might reveal.

In order to deal with the enormous amounts of information our brains receive from our senses, strategies are needed to deal with this to prevent an overload. The human brain does have a remarkable ability to process information but there are biological limitations. Fortunately, unlike computers, the brain does not suddenly freeze and present the message *program not responding* or leave us with a revolving processing wheel and it is able to do this by prioritizing; by almost instantaneously making subconscious judgements as to what needs immediate attention and what can safely be ignored.

How does it do this?

The human brain has evolved to be highly sensitive to change because any change could mean danger and the owner of the brain must be alert to it. One can find oneself sitting staring at a scene passively but the slightest movement caught by the peripheral vision will trigger the brain into a heightened state of alert and the person will turn their attention to the movement for further assessment. If it's the postman walking past, the person will slip back to passive mode but if it's a raging Rottweiler some immediate evasive action might be required.

This sort of evolutionary response has obvious benefits to the survival of the species but the same mechanism is also working during the more mundane parts of life.

Imagine you have a bar of chocolate. The first piece of chocolate you put in your mouth represents a change, the brain focuses on this and the flavor is wonderfully intense but by the time you have reached the end of the bar the taste sensation has become diluted. The first square always has more of an impact than the last square.

When you touch something warm or cool you get an instant sensation, but once your brain is happy it poses no threat you stop noticing it. In other words, the program is always running but sits in the background until called into action. To an extent your computer tries to emulate this; your screen may go into a sleep mode—introduce a change of state by wiggling the mouse and it jumps back into action.

You can probably think of many other examples when the senses become dulled with exposure. It is what is known as the habituation effect and allows people to live by roads with steady traffic without being aware of the constant sound.

Imagine you look at your teacher's face. It is a considerable job for the brain to analyze all the information that comes in from that face and put all the thousands of components together to make a whole. As you continue to look at the unchanging face it would be a dreadful waste of processing capacity if your brain had to constantly reprocess the same information. So it doesn't. It uses the images already stored.

A photographic analogy is useful here. You take a photograph of your mother and store it on your computer. At a later date you want to see a picture of your mother. You either go and take another photograph and download the new information to your hard drive or, much simpler, you can call up the image you already have.

This is what your brain is doing which means the teacher's face you are looking at is not actually strictly speaking the face that is actually there. It is the image of that face your brain has stored. The same is true of your whole environment; thus, you are not experiencing much of the world directly but, rather, you are experiencing the world through your brain's prior knowledge.

An infant's brain doesn't have this prior knowledge and so must work extremely hard to process the world where everything is new and just as it takes time to defragment a file-laden computer the infant's brain needs time to file and organize new information, hence their propensity to sleep a lot.

Of course, the brain is always highly sensitive to change and when one happens it will reprocess the area of change. A tiny change in your teacher's facial expression; the raising of an eyebrow, will trigger the reprocessing of the said eyebrow.

If you find it hard to believe that your brain makes things up, think of blinking. A blink takes around a third of a second and during that time no signal is getting to your brain. There is no light for the eye to process so you would expect to see a momentary period of blackness. Obviously this would be rather annoying so your brain uses the information it already has to predict what will be there during the blank and it fills in the gap seamlessly but it does mean a discrepancy between what you actually see in terms of light coming through your eyes and what you perceive as the image in your brain.

Visual illusions are a reminder that even when the brain is focused it can be fooled. There is no problem with the data the brain receives nor with the brain's ability to process that incoming data but that processed light is not actually what we perceive. The brain wants to make sense of the information before it allows you have the experience of seeing, so what you think you see is not so much what is out there but rather what is in your head.

It can be assumed that the brain is good at extracting sense from information most of the time. Sometimes it gets it wrong but how much is wrong another matter.

The stage illusionist is more concerned with what is not seen. It is there but he doesn't want us to see it otherwise the trick would seem unspectacular. So, he creates changes that will focus the brain's attention and since the brain responds in the same manner, a whole audience's attention can be diverted from where the actual trick is taking place. The brain hasn't so much been fooled, rather it has been persuaded to look in the wrong place. If you look for your shirt in the sock drawer it won't be found.

It seems that the way the world is perceived is not always what is actually there. It might not always be wise to believe what you see.

Think About It

In pairs take an object. One of you is going to argue that the object must be there because you can see it. The other will argue that we cannot be sure.

Discuss your points with a partner.

As a whole group bring your points together. Draw a line showing the poles of the discussion. At one end write *We can believe what we see* and at the other *We cannot believe what we see*.

As each person makes a point, place an arrow on the line showing where the group, as a consensus, lies. The arrow may well move as new points are introduced.

If we cannot assume that truth lies in what we see what implications might this have for society?

THINK—write down your thoughts.
PAIR—discuss what you have with a partner.
SHARE—tell the whole group what ideas your partner had.

Chapter 6

No Future

Few have explored the future in the way Ragit Tagore did in eighteenth century India. As a young philosopher he had often pondered the nature of the future and had often heard his strict father demand that he study hard so as to secure a prosperous future for himself and his family. But Ragit had seen friends do little work yet they walked into prosperity and others, whilst diligent in their studies, struggled in poverty, or fell victim to illness.

The idea that hard work had a direct link to future prosperity seemed attractive but he became concerned that this link had no basis in fact or philosophical reasoning. Perhaps it was simply the older generation's way of controlling the next generation; little more than a threat that sometimes bore truth but sometimes didn't.

In his twenty-fifth year he decided to undertake a lifelong experiment. He was not going to attempt to make a future for himself, instead, he was going to let the future come to him.

He announced his intentions to worshippers as they left the temple. "I will sit on the bottom step and will wait for the future. It will surely come to me, just as surely as it will come to you but I will not battle it all my life. I will let it come and like a branch of a tree thrown into the river I will move as it wishes and I will be carried to the place it takes me."

Five days later, Ragit's body was so dehydrated by the heat of the Indian summer that he fell unconscious and died on the very same step of the temple.

Some hailed him as a great thinker. Others said he was fool, arguing that the future didn't come to him, he chose his own future and it took his life.

Is the future already there, lined up waiting its turn to march into the present? If that were true it would mean destiny has already been determined which, in turn, means you have no control over what happens to you in the future. This is one way of looking at the future but it leaves society feeling very uncomfortable because central to the sense of being is the idea that everyone has some influence over what happens in the future. "Your destiny is in your hands" is a common cry. Take that away and all sense of personal responsibility is removed.

Everyone could do whatever they so wished and claim it was inevitable. People would be no more than actors playing out the future's script. "Don't blame me—it was written in the script of my life," is a cry of defense.

Take exam grades; imagine they are already determined and there is nothing you can do to alter them. Well, you might decide to give up on studying but the fact that you decide to give up studying was also determined. Your choice to give up wasn't actually your choice at all.

Here is another way of thinking of the future: everything that is in the past; all events that have already happened can be visualized as being a rectangular block. On one face of this block lies the present tense. As the present moves into the future the experiences are added to the block so, with time, the block grows bigger and bigger. This is known as Growing Block Theory. The present is there and so is the past but the future has not occurred yet and is the emptiness that lies against the front face of the block, i.e. the present.

In Growing Block Theory there is an assumption that the future is not actually there at the present point, only the present and the past exist. Could it really be that the present is continually being produced out of nothing; that events simply appear out of thin air and jump into the present? This would suggest the future is random and unattached to the present. And one has to ask: where did the present come from?

Consider these examples:

Imagine you make a cup of tea and you have it sitting in front of you. Next, you pick up the cup and drink from it—this was the future event. Was the future event related to the present? Logic would suggest that there is a connection between the present and the future here.

An underwater earthquake (present) causes shock waves which may lead to a Tsunami (future). Again, it would be hard to imagine these events are not related. The future event—the Tsunami seems inevitable.

Hold a tennis ball. Let go (present). It falls to the ground (future). Did the fact that the ball fell appear out of randomness or was it inevitable? Was it linked to the present event?

Investment bankers and those in the insurance industry are people whose livelihoods depend on their ability to see how the future may be linked to what is happening at present. Their job is, literally, to see into the future. If the future were completely random their efforts would be futile.

So, there is a dilemma. Society likes the idea that everyone has self-determination, yet many of society's structures depend on the future being there in some form. Complex patterns such as the stock market or weather patterns may, and do, throw up surprises from time to time but we can explain this in terms of our lack of knowledge, i.e. the patterns are so complex we do not understand them and therefore their connection to the future isn't so clear but it does not mean they are not connected to the future. Only human understanding is lacking.

On a final note, some thinkers take the idea further and claim there is no past and there is no future. The present that is experienced now is the only thing that can be truly called real. But this leads to a problem: by the time an event is experienced in the world it has already passed so it cannot be said that experiences right now are actually in the present. The human sense of the present is actually in the past.

If the present is the only thing that exists in time and it cannot be experienced directly, does that mean nobody can be sure that their experiences are real?

Think About It

If it is assumed the future is determined what things and attitudes in society would change? Write down your ideas.

Would people's lives be easier or more difficult if this were true?

Arrange the class into two—those who think life would be easier if the future has been determined and those who think it would be harder. Stand at opposite sides of the room. Take turns and see if you can persuade others to either join your group or if you make them less sure of their stance they might take a step closer to your group.

What did you think you knew about the future?

Write down your ideas and share them with a partner.

Challenge your ideas.

Highlight those ideas you have that you would now question.

What questions do have now that you didn't have before?

Chapter 7

A Red Sock?

A few years ago Dr. Holden was attending a conference in New Delhi where he had to deliver a short talk to an audience of around two hundred people. On the morning of the talk he woke up in his hotel and turned the light on. Nothing happened. He'd heard that power cuts were a fairly commonplace event and concluded that the great tangle of overhead wire he could see from his hotel window had failed. Perhaps not surprising since he'd seen monkeys use the wires as the equivalent of urban vines.

He opened the curtains wide and let in what little light there was. New Delhi's foggy sunrise was just beginning and gave him enough light to fumble his way round the room, have a shower and retrieve his clothes from his previously unopened suitcase.

He arrived at the venue for the talk and took his place on a chair on the stage along with his two fellow speakers. He noticed a few people in the front rows whispering to each other, looking in his direction and then clearly finding something amusing. Suddenly, alarmed that his greatest fear of standing talking with his zipper undone was about to become a reality, he surreptitiously checked that his zipper was done up. It was. He gave his talk and thought nothing further of the audience's amusement.

He returned to his hotel and decided to change and shower before dinner. It then became apparent what the source of the amusement was: he had one gray sock on one foot and one bright red sock on the other. Naturally, he decided to blame the power cut for this sartorial mishap, rather than his own stupidity.

When light hits an object wavelengths of the light spectrum are reflected back. The colors seen are dependent on the wavelengths that have been absorbed by the object and those that are reflected back. A blue sock reflects different wavelengths from a red sock and the brain perceives them differently: one blue, the other red. It makes perfect sense to refer to one as a red sock and the other as a blue sock.

Everybody has, at some point, woken up in the middle of the night, looked around, and everything has appeared to be shades of gray. Where have the colors gone? This grayness occurs because there is not enough light being reflected off the objects in the room for the person to be able to perceive any color. If you cannot perceive the presence of a ghost you might be happy to say they don't exist. So, in the same vein, if you are unable to perceive colors in dim light are you equally happy to claim they don't exist?

Taken a step further, if all light sources are removed there is no light there to reflect off the object and therefore it cannot be seen at all. Other senses could be used to identify the presence of an object, that is, its shape and texture could be felt, a perceiver may be able to smell, hear or even taste the object but it cannot be seen and its color cannot be identified.

Only the five senses can determine whether anything exists, so it follows that if the senses are removed things may still exist but there is no way of knowing if an object is there. It is possible that space in the world is shared with thousands of spirits but humans simply don't possess a sense to detect them so there is no way to establish whether they exist or not. It is conceivable that other creatures have other senses we don't have and experience the world in a way we cannot.

Back to the Dr.'s sock. If there is no light does the object still have the properties of color? When he places a red sock in his drawer he can see its qualities of redness but when he closes the drawer and any light source is removed from the object, does the sock still possess the qualities of redness? Can he legitimately call it a red sock when in a closed drawer? Of course, it could be argued that the sock nor any other object for that matter possesses a property of color. The color lies in the light and our perception of it, not with the object itself. All objects are black and white. It is the human brain that adds the color.

Could an object have two conflicting properties at the same time? Can a sock have the properties of being red and, at the same time have properties of not being red?

Think About It

Colors only exist when there is light present.

Read the statement above and write down whether you think it is a true or false statement.

A bee "sees" using ultraviolet light. What looks like a yellow flower to you may appear purple to the bee, therefore, a flower can have more than one color at a time depending on who or what is looking at it.

Read the statement above and write down whether you think it is a true or false statement.

Can you apply similar arguments to the other senses?

Working in small groups, write down statements for each sense. Pass them to another group and ask them to state whether they believe them to be true or false.

Chapter 8

The Present

The past, present, and future appear to be integral parts of the way humans experience life and the structure of language allows events that happened in the past to be expressed whether that be a second ago or millions of years ago.

Consider the sentences that express past events.

I have just typed this sentence.
Dinosaurs roamed the earth.

Future events can also be expressed.

I am going to open my mail.
It will snow next week.

The past and future don't appear to present any perplexing problems but the present is a different issue although it might appear to be the simplest as it has only one time frame which is *now*.

The question is: can an event that is happening now actually be experienced? The answer would seem to be a very obvious *yes*. But there are some problems: Imagine you are listening to a song and right now, at a present point, you hear the word *together*. As soon as you have heard the word it becomes an event that happened in the past. Indeed, you would not be able to say that you were hearing the word *together* if the event had not already taken place. This idea can be taken further by breaking *together* into its syllables *to geth er*. By the time the perceiver hears the *geth*, the *to* part has already happened and has become past. In other words, as the word is spoken it trails into the past tense.

Of course the same idea can be taken further by analyzing the initial *t* sound. Although it is a short sound it does have a start and finish and therefore has a time span so by the time the listener has heard the end of the *t* the start of it has already happened and is in the past.

It should be obvious that it is possible to continue breaking aspects of the word down to infinitely small time parts with the same effect occurring. So it would appear that the present cannot have a place in perceived time because it would always have a start and a finish and the start would always go to the past before the finish arrived.

The brain is certainly a very fast processor but the act of processing does take time from the moment a stimulus connects with one of the senses. In fact, the brain becomes aware of a stimulus before it allows the person to become conscious of it. Of course, it also takes time for the event to reach our senses. Anyone who has seen a fighter jet flying overhead knows there is a considerable time lag from the occurrence of the sound to it reaching the ears. The time for the light reflected off the aircraft is much less given that light travels faster than sound but there is still a delay even if it is a very short one.

Subconsciously this is often acknowledged in the use of the present continuous tense.

I am opening the window.

It implies the action is taking place over a time span acknowledging that the action has a past and future component and somewhere within that lies the present.

When a photograph is taken, the image results from the light which hits the sensor. But the shutter may be open for around a one-thousandth of a second so the image is made up of not one instant but one-thousandth of a second. Somewhere in the image the present may lie but without the time frame of one-thousandth of a second there would be no image. The photograph seen is not an image of the present—it is the image of a short span of time.

The sense of the past and future are time related. But where, in that, does the present take its place? Can it only exist in the context of the past and future or can it occupy its own space? If it does, it appears it must do so in an impossibly tiny space of time. Modern day physics can explain much of the world but it is unable to shed light on the present. The present must be shorter than the time span of an instant and physicists cannot make sense of that fact.

No matter what, given that it takes time for a stimulus to reach our senses and it takes the brain time to process the input, by the time a person is consciously aware of the event it has already happened. It follows that the present can never be experienced directly but since the past and future depend on it, it must be there—somewhere.

Think About It

Read the chapter carefully.

Write down three words, two phrases, and one sentence from the chapter that capture the essence of what you have read.

Come together in groups of four or five and record your words, phrases, and sentences on a large sheet.

Each person should explain why they chose the words they chose giving the others the opportunity to challenge or question their choices.

As a group, generate a sentence starting with: *We wonder*....

Each group should share their wonders with the class.

Chapter 9

The Me Gene

Everyone has a chance to say what they want on Hyde Park Corner. Often there are short political speeches, calls for everyone to go to worship, protestors standing up for the rights of snails, comedians looking to cheer up their commuting listeners; sometimes it is garbled nonsense and sometimes thought provoking. What follows is an extract from Danny Daws's minute on the box:

I have some idea of what it feels like to be me though it is difficult to explain to anybody else. And, I'm almost as certain that you have a feeling of being you. I have often asked people, "What does it feel like to be you?" Usually, I get a strange look followed by, "I don't know. It just feels like this," as they wave their arms around.

I know what it feels like to exist and am sure it is independent from my body. I could have an arm amputated and I'd still have the same feeling. I could be blind or deaf or lose my sense of taste and smell and touch but I'd still have a feeling of existing.

I often find myself sitting on the underground looking at the person opposite me and I wonder what it would feel like to be them. I am not talking about their histories or the worries they carry with them or the memories they have of their lives. Leaving all that aside do they have the same feeling of existing that I have? Of course, I am aware that it's an answer I'll never know but that makes me wonder all the more.

Imagine the body being a taxi with you inside. It transports you through life. What if you could stop the taxi, get out, and get into somebody else's taxi? Well, that would let you know what it would feel like to have a different body which would be interesting in its own right but you would still be you.

In order to have the experience of being somebody else it would require you to relinquish your youness meaning you would not be able to experience it directly. So, how to experience being someone else whilst still being yourself and therefore being able to acknowledge the experience remains a perplexing puzzle. Perhaps I need to stop staring at people on the underground.

Have you ever wondered what it is like to be somebody else? Perhaps you have at some time thought, I know what it is like to be me but what do other people experience when they think of themselves? When my friend moves his or her arm do they have the same sensation of possessing an arm as I have? Does their me feel the same as my me? These feelings are known as qualia. Qualia are personal feelings locked inside the individual. I cannot ever explain to anybody what it feels like to be me. I cannot explain what pain feels like or what I experience when I see the color blue—these are qualia. It makes your existence a rather lonely one—you are the only person who will ever know what it is like. We spend much of our conversational lives attempting to convey our feeling to others but we will never actually achieve what we seek. Your mother tells you she loves you and you tell her you love her but neither of you can know what that feeling is for each other so we are left working with assumption that our experiences feel the same. Sometimes when I sit on a bus I look at a person, sometimes old, sometimes young and I wonder what it feels like to be them. Do they have the same sensation of existing that I have, or is it similar, or is it completely different?

What is meant when the word *me* is used? When you say the sentence: *Give it to me*, you are not really saying, give it to my body. Can you express the sentence in a different way without using the word *me*?

With the exception of some of the higher apes and dolphins, animals do not appear to have any concept of *me-ness* or we could say they have no sense of self. There is a simple way of demonstrating this: If you were to paint your dog's nose red and lead it to a mirror it would not show any indication of surprise. It would not recognize its altered image. It has no sense of *me-ness*.

There is no gene present in its genetic makeup that encapsulates that concept of self identity that humans possess. It could be argued that it is this sense of *me* or self awareness that makes humans largely distinct from the animal world, though not exclusively so. Paint a dot of color on a dolphin's forehead or spray a chimp's hair a different color and both will show signs of surprise and curiosity when shown a mirror suggesting that, like humans, they have a concept of self.

Since genes are replicated from generation to generation mutations or random errors can appear. A photocopying analogy is useful here: copy a sheet of text and it appears identical to the original but when the process is repeated, that is, a copy is taken of the copy, soon errors will become visible. Tiny portions of letters disappear and blemishes appear on the white background.

As genes are replicated they too pick up blemishes, some insignificant others highly significant.

There are just over 40,000 genes in the human genome so some random mutations would be expected to occur over successive reproductive cycles.

Going back in time, it is possible that, through random mutation, a gene appeared that gave its owner a sense of being *me*. This had not occurred before and would have died out had the gene not provided some evolutionary advantage to its owner. If it can be assumed it did provide an advantage, its owner was more likely to survive than others who didn't have the gene. In other words, the gene was selected for and was passed on through generation after generation until the point was reached where those without the gene were at such a disadvantage they died out.

It is easy to see how having a *me* gene would lead to a conscious feeling of self which would be of evolutionary advantage. The more selfish the individual, the more likely they would be driven to secure resources for themselves. Consequently, their chance of survival would be increased and the gene would spread into the next generations.

It then follows that the sense of being *me* originates from the same source gene and that gene could in theory be traced back to that one point; back to that very first genetic mutation. Humans then, share the same *me* gene which could mean that the sense you have of *being me* is identical to the person sitting next to you's sense of *me*.

Could it be that there is actually only one *me* shared by us all? That everybody is one, not actually individuals, but a large collective *mes* functioning as one great organism. It is the unity of mankind. Just as the body is made up of millions of individual cells that work together to form a whole? Think of the human body. It is comprised of billions of cells, each individual in their own right, but working together they make up the impressive biological machine—the body.

Perhaps humans are like those cells, each part of a greater organism.

Think About It

Generate as many questions as you can relating to the concept of *me-ness*. This can be done individually or in small groups. Write your questions on separate post-it notes.

Draw a horizontal line or create a line on the floor. Take one question at a time and decide whether the question is likely to generate further insight, calls for deeper understanding and opens the door to new possibilities of thinking. One end of the line represents no opportunity whilst the other end of the continuum represents great possibilities. As a group decide where on the continuum the question should be placed.

Now place a vertical line on the horizontal continuum. This line will represent how much you as a group care about it; how much it is worthy of extra thought and attention. As a group move each question up or down depending on how important it is perceived to be.

With a partner take turns to explain what you experience when you see the color red or explain what it feels like when you stub your big toe.

As a class, discuss what problems you have when you explore qualia.

Chapter 10

The Infinite Line

As a child, Pietro and his family used to visit his aunt in Buxton in Derbyshire, England, on an annual basis for a long weekend. He loved spending time at the market with his aunt as she bought the ingredients for her unrivaled blackberry pie, riding around the park in front of the Pavilion Gardens, taking rides on the miniature railway, and gathering conkers, new and shiny, out of their spiked shells as they walked back home.

In many ways the best part of the visit was the anticipation of the long five-hour drive. As a seven-year-old, this represented a real journey into places strange and unknown; an adventure as exciting as his imagination could muster. The day before, he would go with his father to the petrol station with his two sisters and they'd choose a tin of travel sweets, fruity and covered in icing sugar, a puzzle book each, and a comic.

The reality of the journey was rather different: after half an hour they had done all the puzzles, usually with the help of the answers at the back, the comics had been read, and the travel sweets had lost their tin-sealed magic. Their cheerful smiles turned to backseat sibling squabbles and restless moans. Pietro's parents had their tolerance tested with the constant question, "Are we nearly there yet?" and the reply of, "Not long now" never seemed convincing.

His mother gave him the road atlas to study and she would call out the names of the places on the motorway turn off signs for him to find on the map. He quickly became bored of this distraction and exclaimed, "This journey is going to take forever."

Looking at a map now, he sometimes wonders if, in some way he was right. Of course, they did arrive, suitably grouchy, and the journey had not lasted forever but the distance was perhaps eternal.

48   *Chapter 10*

Take a ruler and a pencil and draw a line of 3 inches.

This seems to be a very simple task that shouldn't pose any problems or questions but no matter how accurate you think you have been you will not have succeeded in this apparently simple task.

Here is the coastline of the Isle of Man just off the West coast of England.

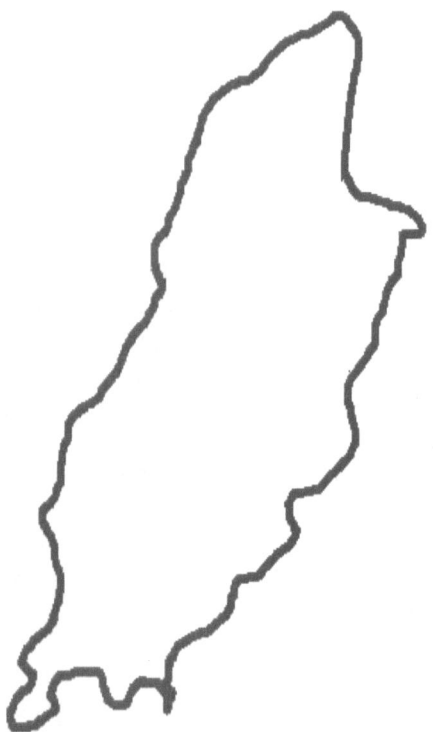

The distance round the coast is approximately 100 miles but the key word here is approximately. If you decide to measure more accurately and you make sure you take your measuring stick round every nook and cranny the result is going to be different. It is going to be longer because you've added in the extra detail.

Now there is a limit as to how accurately you can measure with a straight measuring stick so if you do the same exercise but this time use a short six-inch ruler you can measure more detail. The result? Your new answer is going to tell you the coastline has got longer. If you zoom in even further you could measure round every rock and stone. The result? Your new answer is going to tell you the coastline has gotten longer still. You could go further and measure round every grain of sand and further still by measuring round all the bumps on each grain of sand and every time you zoom in, the coastline is getting longer and longer.

So how long is the coastline of the Isle of Man?

If an infinitely small measuring device was available and infinitely small details were measured the answer would be that it is of infinite length. An infinitely small creature would take an infinite length of time to walk round the coast.

The same principle can be applied to the three-inch line. If you were to look at your *straight* line under a microscope you would see that it is not perfectly straight. There are many very tiny bumps and if each were measured round accurately, the line would not be three inches long. Again, if you had an infinitely small measuring device and measured infinitely small details you would find that your line is actually of an infinite length. So you could conclude that it is never possible to draw a line that has a specified length. Any line you care to draw has infinite length.

This is the principle that lies behind fractals. A fractal occurs when the same pattern is repeated again and again, getting smaller and smaller each time. Nature is full of such examples: look at the veins on a leaf and you see the pattern of the trunk and main branches replicated. Your lungs are similar with the bronchiole branching into ever smaller parts. Even a bolt of lightning splits into ever smaller parts. This principle is often used by computer animators who utilize the computer's processing power to repeatedly generate patterns resulting in landscapes for computer games that look extremely realistic.

Advances in scientific measuring devices allow scientists to see ever smaller worlds but there are limits to what can ever be seen but it doesn't follow to conclude that there is a point at which things stop getting smaller.

Just how small would infinitely small be?

Think About It

On two large sheets of paper write the following two statements:

The line I drew is of infinite length and the coastline of the Isle of Man is of infinite length. The two are of equal length.
 It would take an infinite length of time to travel a distance of infinite length.
 Under each draw two columns with the titles *Agree/Disagree.*
 Give each person the opportunity to say whether they agree or disagree. Each should indicate their strength of conviction using a one to five scale. Give someone who agrees the opportunity to challenge someone who disagrees and vice versa.

Chapter 11

Who Is I?

As a youngster Angelina developed a method of getting out of trouble which confused her parents to the point that they let their accusations drop. A typical scenario would go like this:

"Did you leave the tap on in the bathroom?"
"*You* didn't."
"I know I didn't but did you?"
"But you asked if *you* did it—you said did *you* and I said *you* didn't so I answered."
"Ok then did I do it?"
"I don't know; you tell me."

By this point her parents had got bored with the word play she so enjoyed and found it easier to drop the issue and preserve their sanity. The tap had been turned off anyway so the matter of who left it on in the first place wasn't really relevant. But the question of *who I am*—what is actually meant when a person says "I" is a question that has always perplexed Angelina.

You probably use the simple *I* more times a day than any other word. You put yourself at the center of your world and look at all that happens from your point of view. But what is really meant when the word *I* is used? Just who is *I*?

One of the central themes of Buddhism is the understanding that everything changes all the time. Sometimes those changes are rapid as in when fire turns paper to ash; some are very slow—think of the movements and tiny shifts of the continents that take place over hundreds of thousands of years.

Consider the way the human face changes over time. If you take a photograph of yourself today and another tomorrow will you notice a difference?

Probably not. What if you waited a week or a month? Maybe. Look at a photograph of yourself as a five-year-old and one of yourself now and of course you see the difference. But when did those differences take place?

The answer must be that there are changes every day, in fact every second of every day, but the changes are so tiny that they are unrecognizable to the naked eye. How many of these miniscule changes are needed to be able to recognize a difference is debatable. That a change has happened is not. Like all things, people are changing constantly from second to second.

The same concept can be applied to your brain, your thinking, and your personality. With each experience you have, each conversation, each word you read, problem you solve, your brain has been altered. If follows, therefore, that you are not the same person at the end of the day that you were at the start of it so your *I* that existed when you got up is a different *I* that goes to bed. Your *I* that is there now is not the same *I* as you will have by the time you have finished reading this sentence. The question which arises is: to what are you referring when you use the word *I*? Are people no more than a collection of experiences?

Buddhists suggest that all suffering, however major or minor, hangs on the concept of *I*. Think of how you verbalize your thoughts. *I* am hungry. *I* am uncomfortable. *I* want new trainers. *I* need a mobile phone. *I* am tired.

In all these example *I* is at the center of the thought. Our needs and desires fall away to nothing without *I*. If, as the first half of the chapter suggests, *I* is a meaningless concept then it follows that the needs and wishes of the *I* are equally without substance. Take away the *I* and all suffering will be correspondingly removed.

An interesting consideration is where *I* actually resides. There are three possibilities.

1. Is it just part of the brain's complex chemistry. It follows that with death, the *I* dies with the brain.
2. The *I* lies somewhere out with the brain's chemistry. It is separate from the brain and has no biological or chemical basis itself but it is dependent on the existence of the brain. With the death of the brain it is unable to survive on its own.
3. It lies out with the brain and is totally independent of any biological functioning. When the brain dies in this scenario the *I* is freed and continues to exist without a body.

As with almost all philosophical matters of interest there is no definitive answer. Indeed, that is why they have interested thinkers for thousands of years and will continue to do so. Is a human being no more than a brain; a complex firing of neurons; a brain soup of chemicals and electrical signals; a biological machine? Or, is being human something else; something independent of biology? The scientists will always be frustrated here since no amount of science or measuring or observing will throw out the answer but that does not invalidate the question.

Think About It

Read the following statement:

The *I* that was there this morning is not the same *I* that is sitting here now. Write down what this makes you think and wonder.

Work with a partner. The first person has one minute to speak their responses to the statement. The second person must not interrupt or ask questions. Once the minute is over partners should swap roles.

Chapter 12

What Is an Object?

Harry used to spend hours on the carpet watching his infant son, Max, explore the objects around him. Without Harry's direction he would have found the remote control box or the leg of a chair just as interesting as the pile of plastic toys he placed in front in him in an effort to give his education an early start.

For Max, at a prelinguistic stage of development, objects held a fascination simply because they were there. All were worthy of exploration through the sounds they made, the touch (and hence taste) as explored by his mouth, nose, ears, fingers, and eyes. It was clear that he was using his senses to make sense of the world and the objects that fill it.

But what, exactly, is an object? It might seem like a very simple question. So simple that most never bother to ask it. All sorts of objects fill the environment and are central in every aspect of daily life. Their existence appears so obvious there is no need to define what an object actually is. Most people are happy to accept that something, a pan, a pen, or a shoe, for example, is an object without really knowing what an object is.

Below, are a five properties an object might be considered to have.

1. Objects all exist as individuals. You can point to a particular object and they are concrete, that is, you can see them and touch them. In the language of philosophers, they are concrete particulars.
2. Objects are all time bound. They come into existence, they exist for a period of time, and then, they go out of existence. Take a pencil: there was a time when that pencil wasn't there; it is there now, presently, in your hand but there will be a time when it will not exist anymore. It is, then, possible for a concrete particular to exist and for it not to exist.

3. An object's existence involves change. A block of cheese comes into existence; it changes over time, and eventually reaches a point where it no longer exists.
4. Objects all have a position in space.
5. Objects are made up from parts and each part takes up physical space.

So a pen is made up from the outer shell, the spring, the nib, the ink cartridge, the top, and so on. Putting all the parts together constitutes a pen but it can be surprisingly difficult to say exactly what an apparently simple object like a pen actually is.

Try to think what the qualities or attributes that make up a pen are.

Does it have to be of a cylindrical shape? I have a hexagonal-shaped pen so the answer must be no.

Does it have to be able to write? I have a pen that has run out of ink. Is it still a pen?

Does it have to be made from a specified material? Clearly not—I have plastic ones, metal ones, and even a wooden one.

Is it designed to be held in the hand? If I am using a graphics computer program and use the pen tool, is it a pen?

So what is a pen? Try to devise your own definition and you will find it is surprisingly difficult.

Everything that is understood about the world involves putting things into categories and as humans we are rather good at doing it. People seem to be able to do it without actually being fully aware how they do it. If 500 objects are spread out on the floor and ten of those things were pens most people would have little trouble in picking out the pens; yet at the same time, it is difficult to say what a pen is.

Concrete particulars or objects can be defined in terms of the attributes they possess or the qualities they have. There may be many of these attributes and they can be seen in terms of being parts that make up the whole object. None of the individual qualities on their own can define the object so it is necessary to consider how all the parts or attributes are held together to make the object.

Imagine a simple object like a blue ball. The ball has various qualities. It has a spherical shape, it is smooth to touch, perhaps cool on the skin, it has weight when in the hand, and it has a blue color. Collectively these qualities constitute the blue ball but no individual quality can be said to be the blue ball.

If the blue ball were sprayed with red paint the ball's color would have changed but most would agree that it is the same ball. A person can change their hair color or have a tan but the person remains the same.

Imagine a car drives over the blue, now red, ball and squashes it flat. Most would still agree that it is the same ball even though it has lost the qualities of blueness and roundness.

It is possible to remove all the qualities of the blue ball but somehow the concept of it being a blue ball remains untouched. There appears to be some underlying thing that possesses the qualities. This is what is known as the bare substratum. It is the essential part of the blue ball that possesses the qualities but is independent of them.

Asking a simple question can have surprisingly complex consequences. "What is a pen?" seems simple enough. It is an implement used for writing. It is of cylindrical shape. It contains ink. So what of a pen that is never used, has no ink in it, and is hexagonal? This pen doesn't fit the description of a pen's qualities or functions but most would still agree it is a pen nevertheless.

Try to define a pen and you will find yourself describing its qualities and functions. You can only use the five senses to describe the pen but you cannot actually say what the pen *is*. The bare substratum, that force which hold the concept together, remains elusive.

The problem becomes even more complex when an object is not a single object but a collection of components each with its own bare substratum. Take a car parked on the street. If the windscreen is taken out it is still thought of as a car. Remove the wheels and the seats from the inside, the headlights, and the engine. Most people would still refer to it as being a car. A single wheel axel lying on the road would not be considered a car. As different components are removed there is a point at which it is no longer considered to be car. At what point this occurs remains a mystery and what happens to the bare substratum of the car is equally mysterious. The bare substratum of the car may still be present even though the physical qualities of the car have vanished.

Perhaps it is necessary to go down to the level of the atom. Every object can be seen as having components made from a collection of individual atoms. The properties of a single carbon atom can be described but again, the thing that possesses these qualities cannot. The owner is unknown but as was seen with the blue ball altering the properties does not alter the owner. The owner is the bare substratum or conceptual glue that holds the idea of the object together.

Are you any more able to address the original question—what is an object? Probably not, but you will be aware that there is no simple answer nor is there one correct answer. Indeed, it is an ongoing metaphysical problem but one worthy of thought nevertheless.

Think About It

Think of an object. On your own, take 3 or 4 minutes to generate a list of properties that you think are important in defining the object. You might think of physical attributes and uses.

In a small group take a large sheet of paper and put the name of the object in the middle. Take each of the properties you generated in turn and decide how important each is in defining the object. Those which are most important go close to the object. The least important go at the edge of the paper. You will have to discuss each in turn and reach a consensual agreement.

Next, look at the properties you have spaced out on the paper. If you can see a connection between any of them draw a line between them and write in what way you think they are connected.

When you have finished you will have made a concept map which you can share with other groups. You will be surprised how much debate can arise from trying to define an everyday object.

Chapter 13

Who Are You?

One morning, when Albert was twelve, he got dressed for school as usual, and went downstairs for breakfast. It appeared to be a regular morning. He'd gone to bed at the usual time, read in bed for half an hour, and slept through till his alarm clock informed him of the morning. His mother gave him a slightly strange look when he sat at the table and said, "What on earth were you doing last night?"

Confused by the question as he'd just had a regular night of sleep he said, "Nothing," then added, "Why?"

"What were you doing going round the house putting all the lights on?"

Well, as far as he was concerned he had done no such thing and was perplexed by his mother's seemingly ridiculous suggestion. He was usually more or less happy to admit to things he'd done but this, he hadn't done. "I didn't," he said and turned his attention to buttering his toast.

"You did. You went round and turned every single light on then turned them all off."

"What would I do that for?"

"You tell me. You must have been sleepwalking."

He didn't pursue the conversation as he was rather embarrassed about having done something so bizarre in his sleep and didn't understand whether he should have taken responsibility for this act which was out of his conscious control. He still doesn't know to this day and often ponders the question: "Was it me that did it or was it my brain. Are my brain and me one and the same thing or are they quite separate?"

This question is perhaps as old as mankind and will almost certainly never be answered in the scientific way we have come to expect. It is not possible to complete some research and gather evidence but, because there is never going to be a definitive answer it doesn't mean the question should not be asked.

Possible answers lie in philosophical thought when science fails to give us straightforward, measurable answers.

It is not too difficult to define who you are in terms of your background, your likes and dislikes, hopes and aspirations, but there is a deeper sense that lies under these. People's circumstances can change radically and their outlook and feelings alter with such changes but the inner sense of existing remains constant. Some may be unfortunate enough to suffer life changing injuries or psychological traumas but they always carry the sense of being the same person before and after the event.

Of course, one could argue that the sense of being *me* does change. As a life progresses and gathers experiences and memories, the personal history of the individual changes. The change is constant but an inner sense of self consciousness appears to remain constant or perhaps it simply changes in ways so subtle they go unrecognized.

When you look at a photograph of yourself as an infant it can be hard to imagine that the feeling you have now of being *you* also lived in the child in the picture. If you choose to argue that there is nothing of you left from that time the question: What happened to that *you* needs to be addressed. Did it die? Did it simply vanish?

How would you define who you are?

The most obvious thing to do would be to look at your body in the mirror and think that is who *I* am. But, should you be unfortunate enough to lose a limb or even several limbs or suffer burns or a disfigurement that renders you unrecognizable, your feeling of *me* would still remain. Your hand, for example, is part of your body but that is the end of the relationship you have with it. Your feeling of *me* is in no way dependent on the existence of your hand or on any other outwardly recognizable part of your body.

Before anatomists got to work, the heart was believed to be where the soul resided. Hence expressions like: *I love you from the bottom of my heart* and *a heart to heart talk*. Of course scientists now know the brain is responsible for thinking and reasoning although the mechanisms by which these work are still virtually unknown to neuroscience. It is known that the chemical balance within the brain has a profound effect of behavior. Conditions like insomnia, depression, memory loss, fear, addiction, anger, laughter can all, ultimately, be explained in terms of brain chemistry and the firing of interconnected neurons.

Is *me* no more than a clever bit of brain chemistry?

If all your feelings and emotions were to be altered or removed along with your behaviors and personality traits what would be left? Would your sense of *me-ness* still be there or does it only exist as a collection of past experiences and influences, whether they be social, emotional, or physical? If you choose to believe it would still be there then one must consider the possibility that *me* exists independent of your body's biology and the natural follow-on question is: If *me-ness* has no basis in biology when I die and my body ceases to exist what happens to *me*?

Think About It

Read this chapter carefully.

Write down what concepts are important.

In what way does the text challenge the way you think about yourself? Write down your ideas and share them with a small group.

Does the text change the way you think about yourself or your relationship to others?

On small pieces of paper write points that either support the idea that your brain and you are separate or that they are the same thing. You will probably have ideas that support both points of view. As a class bring the ideas together and sort them according to which view they support.

Is it possible to generate a concluding statement?

What information would you like in order to establish a certain conclusion?

Chapter 14

Not Fair

One day, Ms. Hillstone decided to undertake a small social experiment with her class of ten-year-olds. She split the class into two arbitrary groups. One group was called the Alps, the other the Andes. She informed them that the headmaster wanted to introduce certain changes in the school.

The Alps were to be given three privileges: In assemblies they would be given chairs to sit on while the rest would have to continue, with tolerating, a hard floor. She explained that as there were not enough chairs for everybody only half the class would get the privilege. Secondly, to ease congestion at the tuck shop, the Alps would be allowed to leave classes five minutes early to get their sugary delights, and thirdly, the Alps, as part of an experiment in reducing homework load, would only receive half the amount of the standard homework for the next four weeks.

As she introduced these measures the class listened in stunned silence but on many of the faces of the Andes pupils were looks of utter outrage and they made eye contact with one another to confirm their sense of social injustice. The Alps, on the other hand, smiled at one another and delivered high fives.

It did not take long before one of the Andes said, "That's really unfair, Miss." Others became very vocal in support, "It's unfair, unfair, unfair," they cried in unison.

Not wishing to jeopardize their newly won privileges, none of the Alps pupils made any comment.

Perhaps the Andes were indeed correct in their protestations but why did the Alps group not share their sense of unfairness? What is meant when somebody says something is unfair and where does that concept come from? Can cries of *unfair* be replaced with the words, *I am not getting what I want*? When somebody is getting exactly what they want, almost never will they protest that it is unfair.

How often have you heard people make the claim: *It's not fair* and it often leads to arguments with the person the claim is made against? To be labeled as an unfair person is something we find particularly offensive. Perhaps the reason arguments are so heavily fueled is because there is no common understanding of what is meant by fairness. At a superficial level everybody thinks they know what it means but on closer examination all sorts of issues are raised that need to be thought about before mouths are opened and shouts of *Not fair* are heard.

Fairness is a matter of comparison. Something that exists in complete isolation has no concept of fairness. It is a social concept that binds communities to the notion of equality and as such it can be said to be society-specific in the most general sense. Society here may refer to an economic group, a group defined by national or religious terms, a sports group, and so on.

If outcome f happens to person q when an event, e occurs, i.e. $q + e$ leads to f, the same outcome might be expected no matter who person q happens to be. There is an expectation that $2 + 2$ should always equal 4 and this is true because the qualities of 2ness are stable and consistent but the qualities of an event and the qualities of different people are not stable and they are never identical. If they were, $q + e$ would always equal f and complete fairness would be understood by all but a slightly different event $e(1)$ or a slightly different person $(q1)$ is obviously not going to lead to the outcome f but outcome $f(1)$.

Take an analogy from a game of soccer: If you play a computer version of the game and a player (q) is off side and the program detects this (e) the program disallows the goal (f) and no matter how many times this situation occurs the outcome (f) will always be the same. The program doesn't have the ability to be unfair but is a slave to the programmed algorithms that govern it.

Imagine the same situation but with real players: a player (q) is offside and the referee sees it (e). The referee disallows the goal (f) but if e changes so a player (q) is off side and the referee does not see it $(e1)$ the referee allows the goal $(f1)$.

The closer an individual is bound to members of a group or society, i.e. the closer q is to $q(1)$ the greater the sense of *fairness* is experienced. But the same *fairness* becomes blurred when it crosses boundaries.

In rural Africa, a child who has to walk five miles to get water may not consider this unfair if others have to walk ten miles for the same water. In the United States, a child who is dependent on a garden tap for water would consider this unfair when his or her peers have a tap in their house. Typically, they wouldn't indulge in cross-boundary fairness and think, "I am lucky because I have water in my garden and some children in Africa have to walk five miles to get water."

A refereeing decision that is made in the course of a Major League Baseball match may be fair in that context but would be considered inappropriate for a baseball match in the park played by ten year olds. Thus the concept of fairness is largely contained within a group and is dependent on circumstances.

The closer an individual identifies with people in their group the stronger the sense of fairness. To some privileged children they may make claims that it is unfair that they can't own a horse if their close friends, who live in similar economic circumstances, go to a similar school, have parents in similar jobs, and live in the same area, do own a horse. A child living in inner city poverty is less likely to make the same claim.

The fairness of an event can only be truly established when all other factors are identical. If person (A) doesn't complete his homework and gets no punishment and person (B) doesn't complete his homework and gets a detention this is only unfair in the purest sense if everything about A and B is identical. The more differences there are the weaker the claim of unfairness becomes. Indeed, we often try to control this by making claims that make our situation dissimilar to others. A might try to skew the teacher's idea of fairness by saying his mother had been taken into hospital making his situation different to B and hence weakening the link to B in turn, leading to a different outcome.

This suggests fairness is not a static concept. It grows stronger the closer an individual is to members of his or her group. Thus it is not possible to define what is meant by fairness in universal terms. That is, whatever definition is derived it is unlikely to apply to all situations.

Sometimes our concept of fairness is contained within a partnership. For example, p might agree to help q with his homework if q agrees to lend p his computer game and in turn q agrees to lend p a computer game on the condition that p helps him with his homework. Here, fairness has been negotiated. Assuming p and q are similar people living in a shared society they have a common understanding of value and can trade the value of one thing—homework help—with another—access to a computer game. Both parties have the option to adjust or add conditions—p might consider the value of his homework to be worth access to the computer game for two nights or perhaps a week.

In this example, both parties have a sense of control over the outcome but often a third party comes into play and that third party has to be appealed to and negotiated with. It is here that the concept of a desirable outcome and fair outcome are often confused. For example, children aged ten often make the claim that something is unfair when what they really mean is *I am not getting an outcome I like*.

Consider another example from soccer: player 1 tackles from behind in the penalty box and a penalty is awarded. (Note, the values given to the bad tackle and a subsequent penalty are considered equal. Neither the player, nor the referee has the option of negotiation. The negotiation happened at the rule-making stage and by taking part in a soccer match both player and referee have agreed to abide by the results of that negotiation). A few minutes later player 2 commits a theoretically identical offense in the penalty area. The two scenarios might play out in the following way:

(A) The referee awards a penalty against player 2. Player 2 will typically look for as many differences as possible to make the claim that his offense was not the same as player 1's offense but the condition that the offenses were theoretically identical has been established so his claims of difference are unjustified. When his pleas are rejected by the referee he may mutter that it is all unfair. What he really means is: *I didn't get the outcome I wanted.*
(B) The referee does not award a penalty against player 2. If player 1 is interested in fairness he will protest to the referee explaining that his offense was identical to player 1's and a penalty should be awarded. Thus, he seeks a fair outcome even if it is undesirable.

This is a fairly simple scenario involving three people; two players and a third party. Trying to ensure fairness in society where there may be millions of people, none of whom are identical and a third party, the authority figure, to whom the people appeal seems an impossibly complex task.

Fairness is an absolute term. Like death, there cannot be degrees of it. It makes no sense to say something was a little bit fair or nearly fair. Given this condition and complexity of finding a definition, is it possible to have a fair society?

Does an individual have a right to expect fairness?

Who said the world should be fair? On the surface, most citizens will claim they want a fair world and believe they have a right to expect it but again this is often confused with wanting a world where a citizen gets what he or she wants. Does a child who is going on a holiday to Disneyland protest that this is unfair because their classmates are not going? Typically, they do not.

Nature itself doesn't seem to play by human expectations of fairness.

One seed may land in a prime spot and flourish while another becomes instant bird food.

One of a litter may be weaker than the others. Is it fair that they were born in this condition?

One person may be born with a congenital heart condition and another is not. Is this fair?

If it is not fair to whom or what should the aggrieved appeal to in order to rectify the situation?

One person is a faster runner than another. Is this fair?

Would the world be fair if all were born with the same abilities, the same talents, in the same socio-economic circumstance, with the same opportunities, and if so where is the level of equality drawn and who or what should draw it?

Take two people r and s. s is born into extreme poverty and r into extreme wealth; to make things fair should r also have been born into extreme poverty or should s have been born into extreme wealth? We could ask a similar question of health, i.e. is it fairer if we are all born very sick or all born very healthy? Clearly one is more desirable but that is not the issue.

In conclusion it would appear that there are two distinct types of fairness. There is one where we can exert an element of control and one over which we have no control. Both suggest the concept of equality but while the first is theoretically obtainable the second is not.

Think About It

Make a list of ten things that you think are unfair.

Working in pairs choose one of the ideas you generated. One takes the viewpoint that the event is unfair and the other takes an alternative viewpoint. For example: one might take the viewpoint of a child; the other a teacher or player, referee, company, or customer. Each person takes a turn to explain the situation from their viewpoint.

Others in the group should listen to the two points of view. In turns they should express any concerns they have with the views.

As a group, discuss whether there really is a case of unfairness or are opposing views equally valid at the same time?

Chapter 15

Can Altruism Be Genuine?

It is December 22, 1972, and the Roach family have put up their Christmas tree. The string of colored lights was not sufficiently long to decorate their larger than usual Christmas tree so John Roach had bought another set and had set about wiring the two together and with the flick of a switch he exclaimed his amateur electrical wizardry to be a resounding success. The family retired to bed, the seven-year-old twins, Henry and Freddy to their shared room upstairs, and John and Wendy to their bedroom in the downstairs front room.

The amateur wiring was to have tragic consequences. During the night, it is believed the wiring caused a fire and the tree and presents around its base provided a plentiful source of fuel. John and Wendy were overcome by the smoke that billowed through their open bedroom door and the lives of the children upstairs were dependent on the actions taken by a passer-by, a twenty-one-year-old student, David Franks, who noticed the fire. Franks ran into the blazing house and managed to save the children's lives by lowering them out of the window on a rope of tied sheets.

Franks, not surprisingly, was hailed as a selfless hero and as the family were complete strangers to him it appeared that his actions and willingness to risk his own life were entirely altruistic.

To be altruistic is to do something purely for the good of another without any self gain.

Socio-biologists do not believe there is any such thing as true altruism. Biological entities are concerned with one thing, which is ensuring their genes are passed on to another generation and every action an organism takes is geared toward this goal. Actions that appear to be altruistic at face value mask the real genetic intent.

Faced with potential danger or threat, a bee will not hesitate in issuing a painful sting but in doing so it will make the ultimate sacrifice and die. This could be viewed as the perfect form of altruism but looking at it from a genetic perspective gives a different insight. A bee shares genes with those in the hive as they are descendants from the same queen. To maximize the potential of those genes it is in its genetic best interests to give up its own life in order to protect all the genes it shares with the others in the hive. It is a simple matter of mathematics—one set of genes versus hundreds of sets of the same genes.

Most parents would be willing to sacrifice themselves for the sake of their children. We like to think this is because of love but is this *love* just a less scientific way of saying parents, as biological creatures, want to maximize their genetic potential?

Where resources are limited a creature may be better off genetically by ensuring the survival of relatives than by having its own offspring.

Consider it in a mathematical sense. Two birds A and B have four offspring. Bird A has a sibling who is called A(1). Bird A and bird A(1) share half their genes. The offspring of birds A and B will have half the genes of bird A and half the genes of bird B which means bird A(1) shares ¼ of its genes with each of the offspring. There are 4 offspring and 4 x ¼ = 1 so bird A(1) has a genetic interest of 1. Bird A(1) could increase his genetic worth by having his own offspring. If he were to have one offspring his genetic value would be 1 + ½ = 1½ so it would be in his interest to have his own offspring. But if resources are scarce and there is only enough food to sustain four chicks if he adds his one offspring the result may be that none of the chicks will survive. So to serve his best genetic interests he should help to ensure the survival of his brother's four offspring and not have his own.

The same model can be used for human parents. A child with future reproductive potential will ensure the spreading of genes better than ensuring self-survival of a parent with perhaps limited reproductive potential. Genetically, it makes sense for parents to ensure the survival of their children over their own survival as it is evolution's way of ensuring as much of a parent's genetic code survives into future generations as possible.

The question, therefore remains: is parental love no more than a linguistically palatable way of expressing a selfish desire to maximize genetic potential?

What about a simple act of helping a stranger carry their shopping? Is this just pure altruism or pure kindness or is it another strategy for maximizing genetic potential?

By carrying the shopping, an individual may be seen in a positive light or it might even simply make him/her feel good about him/herself. In turn, this may have the effect of making the individual more desirable to the opposite sex allowing him/her greater potential to choose a suitable mate and hence increasing their genetic potential.

It is easy to see how much of human behavior can translate into a subconscious desire to spread genes. The male satin bowerbird knows the female is attracted to all things blue. To ensure its genes make it into the next generation he must find a mate. The female chooses which bird to mate with and naturally seeks a male who is going to be genetically fit and ensure the survival of their chicks. The male who can display the most blue is the one she will be attracted to and he spends much of his time collecting blue objects to put in his nest.

Humans, of course, are far more complex creatures but the same evolutionary principles apply. Clothes chosen in a shop are selected to make the individual feel more attractive and the ultimate goal is to ensure one's genes are passed on. Make-up is worn to attract, wealth and power attract the opposite sex, intelligence is desirable, being good at sport displays a fit body, which is also attractive.

Both male and female seek a partner who is most likely to have healthy genes and who has the resources to ensure their genetic offspring survive so they in turn can produce their offspring. Could it be that all human behavior is simply about ensuring the survival of genes? Is the desire to be attractive, to be wealthy and be surrounded by objects that display this wealth driven by the same force that makes the bowerbird collect blue objects for its nest?

While David Franks' action was certainly commendable a case could be made that suggests by gaining the status of hero he made himself a more desirable prospect for a female. It is unlikely that this would be a conscious motivation for Franks but many of our biological instincts work at a subconscious level.

Society likes its heroes such as David Franks and is uncomfortable with the idea that all its members are no more than walking gene pools whose every action is a subconscious attempt at biological gain. What makes society feel comfortable and what might be true are quite different things.

Think About It

Generate a list of acts of kindness which could be carried out by a person. Once you have 15–20 ideas get a large sheet of paper and write the word *altruism* in the middle. Now sort the ideas you generated by putting those things which demonstrate altruism most powerfully in the middle and those weakest at the edge of the page with the others at graded points in between. If you do this in a small group, you will find some discussion is needed to agree on each item's position.

Look at where the items have been placed and try to make connections between them. For example, some ideas may involve a stranger helping an individual—these could be connected.

As a group or class bring your connections together and come to a consensus as to what makes an action closest to pure altruism.

You might be in a better position to answer the question: does altruism really exist or is there always something to be gained from performing a so-called altruistic act?

Chapter 16

Present Again

The only way of perceiving the world is through the five senses. Just as a computer takes time to process information so the brain does too. To continue the analogy, the brain has to constantly download enormous quantities of information, process it, decide what parts are relevant and what can be discarded. Information is then synthesized and acted upon. Even the world's most powerful computers would struggle to do anything even remotely as complex as this.

Although the brain is wired to cope with this the processing of information it does take time, and research puts it at around one third of a second. Imagine watching an airplane take off and you witness the moment the wheels leave the ground but what you are actually seeing or more accurately, perceiving, took place a third of second prior to your perception. In other words, your view of the present has already become the past.

Consider the wheels leaving the ground. This will be called an event. In the present, the wheels leave the ground but at some point in the past this event was in the future and at some point in the future this event would become past. There is a contradiction here because the past, present, and future appear to exist at the same time. Perhaps the time frame defined by the past, present, and future doesn't actually exist at all.

Looking at it from a different view point assume that an event which was once the future moves toward the present and then slips into the past. If you tell someone your car moves, it is reasonable for them to ask at what speed it moves, that is, how quickly does it get from a point A to a point B. So it follows that it is also reasonable to ask the same question of time: how quickly does something move from the future to the present and to the past?

In order to answer this question, it would be necessary to have another form of time with which the movement could be measured, and if that were possible yet another form of time would be needed to measure the second form and so on ad infinitum thus making the measurement of time impossible. If we assume anything that exists can be measured in some fashion and time cannot be, is it reasonable to conclude that time doesn't actually exist?

Assume all events exist. Imagine your class stands in a straight line with each person representing an event. Starting at the end of the line the first person says their name and so on down the line. The person saying their name can be thought of as representing the present, those who have said their name are in the past, and those still have to say their name are in the future.

The important thing here is that the people in the past and future are there all the time. They exist in a sort of super-present way. They are there but don't occupy the present tense. By thinking of time in this way we can see that it doesn't move as you might think. Only the present does as it sweeps along the events.

As one flicks through the pages of a photo album the photo on the open page represents the present. The photos on the preceding pages and on those that follow are not there in the present but they have not disappeared. They still exist but it just happens they are not the ones being observed.

Time is often thought of as being linear, that is, an infinite line stretching to the past and to the future with the present representing an infinitely small point on that infinite line. If this is the case it could be argued that the present can't exist. The problem with a linear definition is that it presupposes infinity has a beginning and an end but infinity has no size and no duration. A single point, the present, cannot exist within an infinite time. It simply makes no logical sense.

But what if time were circular and not infinite? This time the class stands in a circle and as each says his or her name they become a past event but they also become a future event because their turn will come round again. Looking at it this way it would be possible for the past to be the future at the same time.

Take a given event in history: Barak Obama becoming President is in the immediate past but if time is circular the event also exists in the future. It is not true to say that it existed in the future in the conventional way of looking at time but by considering time in a circular way a present event can exist in the past, present, and future. That is to say any event will happen again and again and again. It is often said "You only live once" but this may not be true—you may live the same life again and again and again, which is quite a thought.

Think About It

Consider the idea that time goes round in circle.
   Use the following four steps to explore your thinking.
   What excites you about this idea?
   What things do you find worrying about the idea? Are there negative aspects to it?
   Is there anything you feel you need to know about the idea and if so, how might you set about finding out?
   What is your current stance on the idea? At this moment do you think it is a true or false proposition?

Chapter 17

Know What You're Thinking?

On his very first day as a classroom teacher of a group of nine-year-olds, Mr. Peterson overheard one boy asking another, "Has anyone ever told you how ugly you are?" As they were supposed to be doing addition at the time the comment seemed random but he suspected it had come about as a result of some brewing conflict. He intervened, called the boy to his desk and asked him why he had said those words. He shrugged his shoulders and said, "Don't know?"

"You must know," Mr. Peterson insisted. But the boy just continued to stare at him blankly. "Well, come on. You must know."

"I don't," he persisted.

At the time, he put his unwillingness to share the source of his thoughts down to a strategy to get himself out of trouble; say "I don't know" enough and eventually the teacher will give up. He did and sent him away with a phrase as banal as his response: "Well don't do it again."

Sometimes Mr. Peterson likes to have a lie down toward the end of the afternoon. Usually this is just for a few minutes but he often finds himself entering an intriguing and always slightly bizarre state of semi sleep. He has some sort of sense of being in control of his surroundings but he finds his mind drifting randomly into different thoughts; dappling in pools of disconnected ideas. It is almost as though he has lost control of his thinking process and instead, his brain takes over and delivers the thoughts it chooses on his behalf. Where these thoughts come from, of course, Mr. Peterson has no idea.

Thinking back to the boy, Mr. Peterson wondered if perhaps the boy genuinely didn't know why the thought had come to him and then, the more he thought about it he wondered if anyone actually knows where their thoughts come from.

Does anyone have their own thoughts or does the brain have the thoughts and then informs the conscious self and only after the individual becomes aware of them?

Any pet owner will often look at their animal and wonder what it is thinking. Of course the idea of a dog thinking thoughts in a series of woofs seems ridiculous but any pet owner will claim their animal has a capacity for thought. So what are they thinking in? Is it possible to think without language? Perhaps it is language that allows the organism to become consciously aware of thoughts but it may not be necessary for the source of the thinking.

Children who have been born totally deaf and have not been taught sign language have given scientists an insight into a world without language. Typically they can solve problems in a way an animal can but their ability to reason is severely limited.

On a daily basis we all solve micro problems without appearing to think. Consider this problem:

I want to drink some water.
I have a glass of water in front of me.
What do I do?

The solution is so obvious that anyone is able to perform the action of drinking the tea without any language processing. The person does not need to think:

Pick up the cup, lift it to my mouth, open my mouth, put my lower lip on the rim of the cup and tilt the cup slightly.

Many daily activities such as getting dressed, opening files on a computer, locking a door, etc. can be performed without any conscious thinking.

Infants enjoy the brain at the peak of its learning ability. In this pre-language state decision making and thinking is clearly possible yet the brain seems to have made decisions without its owner being consciously aware of them. Sadly, the memories of what it is like to be a toddler are lost so the processes or experiences of what is going on in the brain of the infant remain mysterious. It may be that the memories are lost because the toddler had no capacity to encode experience into language.

Higher order thinking is a different matter. Thinking that involves reflecting on the past or on predicting the future requires an element of conscious awareness. So is language needed for this type of thinking?

Can you think what you would like to eat this evening without using language?

You can probably just about manage this using pictures in your mind. It is easy to conjure up an image of a pizza without having to think *pizza*. A dog alone in the house waiting for its owner might rely on a series of images recalled from past, familiar events but it may also be possible to generate images of things that will happen in the future and thus plan ahead in some way.

You may be going on holiday to a new destination but you will probably create detailed images of what you think it will look like. You can use stored images you have of yourself, swimming pools, sun beds, etc. to see yourself, in your mind's eye, lying by the poolside. This form of future planning may be nothing like what actually happens in reality when you arrive on holiday but that is a quality shared by all forms of planning.

Are language and/or pictures always used to think or make decisions? You may be faced with making the decision as to whether to buy a hamburger or a cheeseburger. Can you make a decision without being consciously aware of the mechanisms you have used?

Where do your thoughts come from?

Ask someone to tell you what they did last weekend.

There was probably a fairly steady flow of words. The talker did not have to literally think out the words before speaking.

When you speak are you consciously aware of what words are going to leave your mouth?

Sometimes it seems as if a speaker is able to generate a *flavor* of what he wants to say. Put another way, there is a conscious intention but the actual words used to express the intention seem to be generated away from our consciousness.

Nobody knows exactly what words they are going to say before they utter them; yet they have a sense of what they are going to say. It seems that this process of prethinking happens without language. Imagine you want to go to a party but your mother says you cannot go. You have a sense of how you are going to argue your case but this sense is not internally verbalized. You don't need to think to yourself: *I am going to suggest I should be allowed to go because I will be getting a lift home from my friend's father.*

If the words you utter only become directly known to you after the point of thought generation can you legitimately claim them to be your words or are they your brain's words?

Are they a direct result of your mental wishes or can the words be more accurately described as being the result of a highly complex string of chemical reactions in the brain?

If this is the case the really big question is: can you be held responsible for your words or should the physical brain take the responsibility?

This is a question society doesn't like to address because society is held together by the idea of individual responsibility. If science tells us our thoughts are no more than the results of chemical reactions it is hard to hold anyone responsible for anything. Society is not ready to deal with such a terrifying idea.

Think About It

The task is to capture the heart of this chapter. What are the important aspects?

Write down three words, two phrases, and one sentence from the chapter that capture the essence of what you have read.

Come together in groups of four or five and record your words, phrases and sentences on a large sheet. Each person should explain why they chose the words they chose giving the others the opportunity to challenge or question their choices.

As a group generate a sentence starting with: "We wonder...."

Each group should share their wonders with the class.

Chapter 18

Is Choice a Good Thing?

Last week Harry Hadock was staying in a conference hotel in Amsterdam. On the last evening he decided to stay in his hotel room and have a lazy evening watching some television. He preferred not to have a television at home so he was looking forward to the novelty of watching an interesting program. Picking up the remote control with its bank of confusing buttons, he lay on the bed and flicked the TV on.

It came on as a default on the CNN channel but the item on Wall Street didn't hold his interest for long so he flicked on to the next channel—the Saudi sports channel. He watched two Saudi teams play football for all of about thirty seconds then went on to the next channel. An hour later he'd worked his way through the 200 channels the hotel had to offer and arrived back at CNN not actually having had any satisfying experience. He completed two more cycles and realized he hadn't actually watched anything and wondered if there had been the choice of only two or three channels if he would have settled to a program and enjoyed it.

Would more channels have made his viewing better or easier? He suspected not.

Most people celebrate the fact that the modern world offers us all sorts of choices as it appeals to the nature of the consumer. No longer do shoppers simply have to *make do*. Instead they can pick and choose until they have exactly what they want and the more choice there is the greater the likelihood that they will end up satisfied. That is the theory.

When Harry, as a fifteen-year-old, bought his very first computer there was no choice. He could have had a ZX 81 or he could have had no computer at all. The decision was very simple and he chose the ZX 81. He was delighted with it and never did he have to wrestle with the idea that he should have bought a different model as there were none. Life was simple and straightforward.

Last year and some 35 years later, Harry decided to invest in a new computer. First of all, he had to decide whether to go down the laptop route, or perhaps a tablet would be better, or he could have a tower, or an all-in-one monitor and computer. After much deliberation he opted for the conventional tower.

Next he had to decide on the brand, the type of processor and the storage capacity. Like many, he didn't have a great understanding of processors and their relative merits so he found himself trying to make a decision based on what the strings of numbers and letters looked like. Next, he had to consider the size of RAM he might need and the storage capacity of the hard drive, the color of the computer, the style and type of monitor, and its size. This decision-making process was long and arduous and he often found himself thinking: *I just want a computer.*

He became rather fascinated by the decision-making process he had to go through. He had no idea what the differences between an Athlon II X4 620, an Atom 330 (1.6 GHz dual core) and a Dual-Core T3100 (1.9 GHz dual core) were; yet some force was operating in his mind that made him come to a decision. The force was not one of knowledge or understanding. He felt he was making decisions based on ill-conceived ideas of superiority. Numbers and letters are important here so something labeled GL3x.2 must be better than a GL3x.1 which in turn must be better than a GL3. He was aware that this is a clever strategy used by marketing departments but, at the same time, he knew it is almost impossible to detach oneself from it. His decision, he knew, was not based on logic.

Two weeks after his endless deliberations, his new computer and monitor arrived. He unpacked the contents and connected all of the components. All seemed to work fine but it wasn't long before he began to wonder if he should have opted for the wireless keyboard, perhaps he should have gone for a bigger storage capacity, perhaps the bigger screen would have been more comfortable for his eyes.

He reflected on the time he got his first ZX 81 and recognized that the joy from unpacking wasn't clouded with any doubts. There were no other choices and the pleasure was pure and uncluttered. And that pleasure lasted until the computer had burned out four years later.

Perhaps life would be a lot easier if there were fewer choices. Choices do not offer the freedom they suggest; they draw us into an endless cycle of consumerism: a world where there is a sausage and that is it, instead of having to decide between pork, beef, pork and stilton, pork and apple, beef and mustard, low fat, reduced salt, free range, organic, fat, thin, and then wondering as they sizzle in the pan whether a different choice would have been better.

In a world that seems to be getting ever faster and where a person's time is equated to money one has to question how much time is wasted by people choosing a simple product. If you wanted to buy a camera and were to do your research thoroughly you could spend hundreds of hours reading internet reviews of each model and after having done that you would probably still struggle to make a logical decision.

Young children give valuable insights into the quandary of choice. Give a child a surprise present and she will be happy to receive a new toy. The pleasure is straightforward and the satisfaction genuine. Take the same child to the toy shop to buy a present and she will find herself bombarded with choice. She may spend some time jumping from one desirable object to another. She is thrown into confusion and fears making the wrong decision. In the end, no matter which toy she selects she will be left with that inevitable thought everyone has to live with: *did I make the right choice?*

The difficulty with this question is that it is not possible to ever know the answer. The student who chose to study medicine over engineering will never know what her life would have been like had she chosen the other and, therefore, has no mechanism for evaluating the success of the decision. The more choice there is in society the more unanswered questions everyone has to accept.

Think About It

Imagine you want to buy a portable device to listen to music on. Make a list of everything that will be important in making a final decision.

In small groups, compare lists and generate one for the whole group.

On a large sheet of paper write *portable music player* in the middle and draw a box round it. Take each item on your list, one by one, and decide where it should be placed depending on its importance. Things the group decides to be most important in the decision-making process should be written close to the center box while things of least importance are placed toward the edges of the paper.

Now look for connections that exist between your ideas. If your group agrees there is a connection, draw a line between the two things and write in what way they are connected along the line.

Share your finished diagram with others in the class and discuss any similarities or differences you notice.

Chapter 19

Is Anything Random?

As a teacher, Sandra Friedmann has often made simple addition worksheets for her pupils. She sits down and thinks of two random numbers under one hundred for them to add. Very quickly she becomes aware that the same numbers seem to keep reappearing, or she thinks, *The last number I chose ended in a 5 so I can't do that again.*

What started as an exercise in random generation quickly became a deliberate and calculated attempt to choose a range of different numbers. Of course, there was a logic to her deliberate interference with the randomness because she wanted to ensure the pupils added a range of different numbers.

An interesting exercise to try is to think of a coin toss. Imagine you have to predict the results of 100 tosses and, using a computer, type an H for heads and T for tails as quickly as you can. Very quickly you will observe that you are not typing randomly and you start thinking, *I've done five Hs in a row so now I need to do a few Ts.* Of course what you are trying to do is make the string of letters random but in the act of trying, by definition, your letters lose their randomness. It appears there is a conscious mechanism in the brain which prevents randomness.

A computer, given the same task, doesn't have the conscious element people have and so the string of letters appears to have genuine qualities of randomness. If the computer generates an infinite string of two letters, mathematics predict that exactly half will be Hs and exactly half will be Ts. Although each individual throw has a random outcome, the laws of probability inform us that the combined results of many throws will follow a predictable result.

Of course, the computer can only generate so-called random events if the algorithm it has been programmed with permits randomness. Since an algorithm is essentially a mathematical rule it is not truly random. A rule cannot have randomness otherwise it wouldn't be a rule. It seems reasonable to conclude that the computer, like people, is incapable of genuine randomness.

Imagine there is some way of generating truly random numbers, the laws of probability predict the outcome of 50:50. But the fact that the results follow some predetermined law bring the concept of randomness into question. Each individual toss of a coin may be random but the total of an infinite sample can be predicted by a mathematical law. However, the infinite sample is a concept and can never actually exist which means the predictability of the law is also conceptual. It is difficult to see how individually random events can ever total an outcome that is not random.

A distinction must be drawn between randomness and unpredictability. Weather patterns for example are notoriously hard to predict since a small movement of air on one side of the planet may eventually have an impact thousands of miles away. Although hugely complex calculations test even the world's most powerful computers, there is, theoretically, a possibility of accurate prediction because the patterns are not random but follow known laws of physics.

There is a tendency to apply the word random to events where there is no way of predicting outcomes but because events may be beyond the realms of human explanation it does not mean the outcomes are actually random. There may be a pattern simply waiting to be unlocked.

As already stated, a computer generating a random number operates under an algorithm which must necessarily be bound by rules dictated by the programmer. Since the rise in popularity of lotteries that offer enormous payouts to those who pick the chosen numbers, everyone from scholars to astrologers have attempted to find a pattern in randomness of the numbers selected by computers. As yet nobody has managed to find a pattern but to say there is *no pattern* is very different from saying *no pattern has been found*. The search continues in earnest.

Mathematicians are pattern hunters and for centuries have been fascinated by prime numbers and Pi both of which appear not to follow a pattern. It is possible that the pattern is random but mathematicians don't believe this. There is a pattern to be found, it is just that nobody has found it yet.

Many religions reject the idea of randomness believing that everything is part of a complex plan, the workings of which we have no access to. They share this belief with scientists and mathematicians although they differ in terms of who or what is master of the plan.

Are the random genetic mutations biologists often refer to really random or they part of a greater plan which is beyond our understanding?

And what of the so-called *free will* that defines human beings? If every thought you have is somehow connected with previous thoughts, experiences, or events, then your ability to generate a random thought doesn't exist as it must be dependent on a prior event. Free will must also be dependent on the past and as such isn't nearly as free as people would like to believe.

Perhaps it is possible to take any thought and trace its origins back to some starting stimuli. How these stimuli are encountered might be random and out of our control and how that very first event came into being is another matter for thought. Someone might witness a person being attacked by a dog and later find himself thinking of teeth, then make an appointment with his dentist. The thoughts that followed the stimuli (the dog attack) are not random but the fact that he happened to be in a place at a given time and this led him to encounter the incident may be random. Or perhaps not, since his position in space must also have been linked to previous events.

The idea that an event can simply appear out of random thin air seems improbable. If you hold a ball in your hand and you announce that you are going to drop it, the fact that it will fall to the ground is not random but dependent on the past event of you letting go of the ball. The ball may roll, causing another event which in turn causes another event and so on. This linking of causes will go on indefinitely so in a hundred years some event could be linked all the way back to the dropping of the ball.

Those who choose to believe in fate believe it to be part of a greater plan over which we have no control. Fate, however, is not random. It is pre-planned. By whom? The example of dropping the ball suggests that events in the immediate future are linked to ones in the immediate past but how far can this time frame be extended?

Sandra met her husband in an airport departure lounge while waiting for her delayed flight. Had her flight not been delayed she would never have met him and their three children would never have been born. Were all the events from the point at which they met and before randomly organized or were they all connected? If all events are connected they become predictable. The tools of prediction may not exist but they are predictable nevertheless.

If a ball is dropped onto the floor its precise resting position can, in theory, be precisely predicted. There are many factors to consider: the height the ball was dropped from, the microstructure of the ball's surface and the floor's surface, the movement of air particles, and so on. There are too many factors interacting in complex ways for the exact location of the ball to be predicted but there is always a difference between what is possible and what humans at this point in history can do. If it were possible to understand how each of billions of neurons firing in the brain were connected to each other it might be possible to predict exactly at what point in history the resting position of a falling ball could be calculated.

A few days ago Speth Lee was sitting in an Italian restaurant. The waiter brought the menu and Speth spent some time wondering whether he should have the spaghetti carbonara or a pizza. It is hard to understand what is actually happening during this process of wondering but in the end he chose the pizza. Of course, Speth liked to believe he was master of his own destiny. He could have chosen the spaghetti if he had wanted to. It was his choice. This idea that everybody has choice is so central to our existence it is rarely challenged but what if it is not true?

Looking at the menu starts a complex triggering of neurons in the brain. Like the ball, the end result is predetermined. The process of thinking and making a decision is only part of the neural bouncing process in the brain. Of course, it is more complex bouncing than the ball but bouncing it is nevertheless. So, just as the ball was always going to land in position x, Speth's neurons were always going to make him arrive at the choice of the spaghetti. He couldn't have chosen pizza. Put simply, it was never going to happen because the neurons in his brain hadn't gone down the pizza path.

As our understanding of neuroscience grows, it seems that this may well be the way in which the brain functions. It does leave people feeling rather uncomfortable though; if you have no real choice can you ever be held responsible for anything you do? You can say, "It wasn't my choice, it was simply the decision my brain landed up on."

Whether you decide to give up on making choices or not is of course not your choice! It would seem there is no escape.

Think About It

Write down what you think the word *random* means. Give several examples of events that might be considered to be random.

How does the reading of the passage change what you knew or thought you knew before? Pupils should record their individual responses and then discuss them in groups.

Reflect on how your previous views have been altered or extended and record what you wonder about now.

Discuss these as a class and explore possible ways in which you could satisfy your wonderings. Do you think it is possible or does thinking more about a topic simply open up yet more wonderings?

Chapter 20

The Bare Substratum

Bertie was old and spent most of his days lying sleeping on the shelf above the radiator occasionally opening a feline eye to observe the comings and goings in the kitchen. Tina loved to sit by him while her mother cooked dinner and stroke the line from his nose over his head and all the way back to his tail until his purr was deep and comforting.

One afternoon Bertie didn't purr. His breathing became erratic and he spluttered and coughed. Tina stroked his head but his eyes didn't close softly with the comfort he usually felt from her touch. Her mom made an emergency appointment with the vet and Bertie was placed in his carrier box. Usually he would have struggled and resisted but his body was limp and tired. When she returned an hour later her eyes were red and the box was empty.

"Bertie's gone to a very peaceful place now," she told Tina.

"You mean Bertie's dead?"

"He was old, Tina. And you saw how sick he was becoming. He's not suffering anymore."

"But he's dead," Tina cried and ran up to her bedroom where she lay, her head buried in tears and pillows.

When the sun had gone down behind the hills and the sound of sobbing had stopped, Tina's mom went into her daughter's bedroom and sat on the edge of the bed. She pulled the covers back from Tina's face and placed her open palm on her cheeks and stroked the tear stains away with the tip of her finger.

"I know it's sad. We are all sad, Tina. But Bertie was very old and he was suffering. He's at peace now."

"Is he in heaven?"

"Yes and he's still here with us. Not his old cat body but his spirit is still here. Right here in this house just like always."

"Do you think he'll still meow at the end of my bed every morning."

"Well, you never know. If you listen very carefully you might just hear him."

The idea of there being something separate from the body, a spirit or soul is an idea that is as old as Man himself and has been explored in volumes of religious and philosophical works. But what about an object? Is there any way it can also be considered to have a spirit; some binding force that has no physical presence?

Imagine a simple object like a blue ball. The ball has various qualities. It has a spherical shape, it is smooth to touch, perhaps cool on the skin, it has weight when in the hand and it has a blue color. Collectively these qualities constitute the blue ball but no individual quality can be said to be the blue ball.

If the blue ball were sprayed with red paint the ball's color would have changed but most would agree that it is the same ball. A person can change their hair color or have a tan but the person remains the same.

Imagine a car drives over the blue, now red, ball and squashes it flat. Most would still agree that it is the same ball even though it has lost the qualities of blueness and roundness.

It is possible to remove all the qualities of the blue ball but somehow the concept of it being a blue ball remains untouched. There appears to be some underlying thing that possesses the qualities. This is what is known as the bare substratum. It is the essential part of the blue ball that possesses the qualities but is independent of them. It is the thing that holds the idea of the ball together.

This may seem like a bizarre idea but a person changes constantly throughout life and most are happy to believe the person is the same person. Both the outward appearances can change and the personality evolves but Tina's mom who is now 41 years old is the same person she was when she was a little girl.

Asking a simple question can have surprisingly complex consequences. *What is a pen?* seems simple enough. It is an implement used for writing. It is of cylindrical shape. It contains ink. So, what of a pen that is never used, has no ink in it and is hexagonal? This pen doesn't fit the description of a pen's qualities or functions but most would still agree it is a pen nevertheless.

Try to define a pen and you will find yourself describing its qualities and functions. You can only use the five senses to describe the pen but it is impossible to say what the pen actually is. The bare substratum, that force which holds the concept together, remains elusive.

The problem becomes even more complex when an object is not a single object but a collection of components each with its own bare substratum.

Take a car parked on the street. If the windscreen is taken out, it is still thought of as a car. Remove the wheels and the seats from the inside, the headlights and the engine. Most people would still refer to it as being a car.

A single wheel axel lying on the road on the other hand would not be considered a car.

As different components are removed, there is a point at which it is no longer considered to be a car. At what point this occurs remains a mystery and what happens to the bare substratum of the car is equally mysterious. It is possible that the bare substratum of the car may still be present even though the physical qualities of the car have vanished.

Perhaps it is necessary to go down to the level of the atom. Every object can be seen as having components made from a collection of individual atoms. The properties of a single carbon atom can be described but again, the thing that possesses these qualities cannot. The owner is unknown but, as was seen with the blue ball, altering the properties does not alter the owner.

Tina's mom may be correct. Bertie's body and Bertie's qualities have gone but the owner of the body and the qualities, Bertie, may still be there. His body died but he didn't.

Think About It

Consider the following statement:

When a person dies the body disappears with time but the person is still there.
Use the following four elements to explore your thinking.
What excites you about the statement?
What worries or concerns would you have if the statement is true?
What further things would you need to know in order to establish whether the statement is true or not?
What stance are you going to take on the statement? Think how you can justify your reasoning.
As a group share your thinking.

Chapter 21

Infinite Universes

For his 13th birthday, Kebu was given a telescope. He hadn't previously shown any interest in the night sky but his family had recently moved to the countryside. Free from the light pollution of any big city, the night sky became a source of fascination. He moved his bed so it was next to the window and at night he would often open the curtain and simply stare into the inky night. It seemed to him that the longer he looked the more stars appeared as minute pinpricks of light.

"Each one is a sun very much like ours," his father told him.

"Do they have planets like ours?"

"Some do. I'm not sure scientists really know much about what is out there."

"Maybe there is one out there that is same as ours."

Kebu unpacked the telescope and set it up in the shed in the garden. That way he could sit in warmth and scan the stars and look for a planet like earth. He told his classmates what he was doing and they laughed at him. "There is no other planet Earth," they said.

"But nobody knows what lies beyond the farthest stars. There must be more and more and somewhere there might be another planet just like this one. Maybe it even has me and you on it."

The pupils laughed and told him his mind was full of fantasy. "You're an idiot. You don't know anything," they told him.

His teacher was a mathematician and was interested in his idea. "Oh, and you lot know everything, do you?" he said pointing his finger at the rest of the class.

At recess, the teacher went to the preschool department and borrowed a box of Lego play bricks and in the next lesson he handed out four bricks to each pupil in Kebu's class and asked them each to fix the four blocks together in any way they wished. Once they had completed the task he collected the models and set them out on the table.

"Do you notice anything?" he asked the class.

One boy pointed to two of the models and said, "They are all different except for these two. They are exactly the same."

"And why do you think that happened?" he asked.

"Because there is only so many things you can make with four blocks so eventually some are going to be the same as others," Kebu said.

"Correct. Now imagine our planet and everything on is made from Lego blocks. There are trillions upon trillions of them all arranged in the one way that makes everything as it is now. Imagine we take all the blocks apart and rearrange them. We will make different planets and different stars and different universes but if you keep rearranging and rearranging eventually they will be put together in exactly the same way they are in our universe right now. This is a mathematical certainty. Every detail will be identical. There will be another you and you and you," he said pointing to the pupils who stood in wonder at the possibility. "They will even have the same thoughts and the same memories."

"And there is more," he went on, "if space goes on for infinity then it follows that there must be an infinite number of planets identical to ours. There is not just one or two of you but an infinite number of yous floating around out there in space."

That night, Kebu set up his telescope and when he peered into the distant night sky he was sure he could see another plant with another Kebu looking back at him through his telescope.

At the end, it would appear that Kebu's imagination was taking over but his teacher's logic made perfect sense. It follows basic principles of probability. To challenge the teacher's thinking would be to challenge all that mathematical probability can prove to be mathematically true.

The idea of there being multiple and identical universes may be a difficult and uncomfortable concept to wrestle with but quantum physics adds another perplexing dimension to the question.

In theories of quantum mechanics, it is possible for a particle to exist in more than one place at a time meaning the same particle can exist in two different or parallel universes. Imagine a simple scenario where a particle can move either to the left or to the right. In quantum mechanics, the particle may go left into a new universe but the same particle can also go right into another new but different universe. With each alternative, the particle doesn't, in effect, have to choose because it can simply enter both worlds. The worlds are different but it is the very same particle in both.

Now imagine the same principle applied to all the particles that make up Kebu. When Kebu has a decision to make he appears to make one choice and this is the world he lives in. But, if quantum mechanics is true, he also makes the other choice and the same Kebu also lives in that world and his life thereafter, in both universes will take different courses.

If, every time, there is a decision to be made he splits and exists in both worlds, with time, he will exist in an almost infinite number of different, parallel universes. Of course he is consciously aware of the universe he is in but the same Kebu is consciously aware of being himself in each of the parallel universes. He has the feeling that the universe he is experiencing now is actually the real one but all the other Kebus in all the other universes also have the same feeling.

To many this seems like a wild science fiction fantasy but new understandings of mathematics and physics must make the open-minded thinker question what has been taken for granted in the past even if it leaves our sense of identity in a very confused place.

Think About It

Imagine you could talk to a copy yourself who lives in a parallel universe. What might you want to ask them? What, logically, would they ask you?
  Write down your questions and share them as a class.

If you could choose between parallel universes where there are many *yous* all of whom have made different decisions or ones where there are identical versions of you which would you choose?
  Why do you think that? Explore your ideas in a small group.

Chapter 22

Infinity

The idea of *foreverness* is one which has always fascinated and perplexed humans. On the one hand it appeals to one sense of logic that suggests time and space don't have any boundaries but at the same time another logic would suggest everything must come to a conclusion at some point. If one traveled in a space rocket eventually it would reach the end of space but there must be more space beyond. The two ideas are in direct conflict and perhaps provide the greatest source of wonderment of the universe.

Students often marvel at the idea of outer space going on and on but inner space is often neglected in this thinking but is subject to the same basic logic. Take any object, a grain of rice for example, cut it in half and it gets smaller. Take one of the halves and cut it in half and it gets smaller still. There will always be something to cut in half. It seems inner space, like outer space, is infinite.

Humans created a concept they called infinity to try to cope with this conflict but no matter how hard one tries to understand it, it always manages to baffle since its size is perplexing.

What is surprising is that infinity doesn't always appear to be the same size. Take the number sequence:

0 1 2 3 4 5 6..................

This sequence can be carried on for infinity.
Now consider:

0 2 4 6 8 ....

This sequence can also be continued until infinity but clearly it is half the size of the first infinity.

.... −4 −3 −2 −1 0 1 2 3 4 ....

This sequence can be extended to infinity in both directions so it follows that it must be twice the size of the first example of infinity.

And to make matters more confusing it is generally recognized that there are two types of infinity. The examples above are examples of *potential infinity*. This is the concept Greek philosophers worked with. The sequence 0,1,2,3,4.......... can potentially reach infinity but it will never actually get there since another unit can always be added to the last entry.

A more useful way of considering infinity for mathematicians is to use the concept of *actual infinity*. This differs from *potential infinity* because there is a defined set. In other words, the starting and finishing boundaries are there. Consider the number of fractions that lie between 1 and 2. There are an infinite number but they must all exist within a given set. Although it is not possible to reach the answer there is a theoretical or *actual infinity*.

There is always a tendency to think of infinity in terms of *size*. Instinctually, infinity is thought of as being very, very large but, in truth, infinity is not any size. It is neither big nor small but completely *sizeless* although it can be argued that *actual infinity* has a theoretical size.

If space is considered to go for an infinite distance it actually means space has no size at all. If it is true to say a person was unborn for an infinite amount of time and that they will be dead for an infinite amount of time it must be borne in mind that this infinity doesn't represent a duration of time. It has no size. It has no duration. A million miles or a thousand years may seem large but when they are placed in a context of infinity they have no meaning. Put another way: the measurable has no place in the world of the immeasurable.

Infinity is not a fixed entity but a malleable concept. It is not something that goes on and on and on because that suggests it is going somewhere. It is not. It has no direction. It just *is*. To work with the concept of infinity is to accept its dimensionless form. To attempt to slot it in to an existing sense of logic will most likely leave the most ardent thinker in a state of confusion.

Think About It

At the end of the day everybody goes home. Take an imaginary person, Lena, who plans to walk home. In order for her to get from school to her home she must walk half the distance first. That seems very obvious. Once she has reached the half-way point she must then walk half the remaining distance and from that point, half the remaining distance again. She will have to repeat this an infinite number of times. This means she will continually get closer and closer to her home but she will never actually get there.

There must be a flaw in the logic somewhere since Lena will actually be able to get home.

This is a paradox which fascinated the philosopher Zeno and it is known as *Zeno's Paradox*.

Read *Zeno's Paradox* again carefully in a small group.

Each person should have the opportunity to say what they think about it.

Then each should have the opportunity to say what they wonder.

The paradox comes about if infinity is reasoned to be *potential infinity*. It is where Lena would never get home. Thinking of *actual infinity* allows her to reach her final destination.

Brainstorm for other situations where *actual infinity* makes more sense than *potential infinity*.

Chapter 23

Silence

Redmond Hillary was a happy, active boy who, like all two-year-olds, spent his waking hours exploring the world with his five senses. On the eve of his third birthday he appeared irritable and his cheeks became flushed. His mother put him to bed but he didn't settle, turning and twisting under the covers and his temperature started to rise at an alarming rate.

Just before midnight, Redmond was rushed to hospital. He lay in a critical state for over ten days in an intensive care ward surrounded by flashing monitors, wires, tubes and concerned nurses who monitored all his vital functions. Slowly, Redmond regained consciousness and his organs resumed their essential work without the support of machines. His parents breathed a sigh of relief when he was moved to a low dependency ward.

Redmond was quiet and withdrawn but they expected he'd been left exhausted by the illness and would be his usual self once they got him home. The virus had, however, had a devastating impact of the auditory center in his brain and Redmond was left totally deaf.

Further medical investigation didn't reveal any damage to his ears and to this day they continue to work normally.

In a healthy person, vibrations are relayed through the ear drum into the inner ear where the cochlea transfers the vibrations into electrical signals which then travel along the auditory nerve to the brain for processing. Redmond's brain receives the signals but the processor is damaged and he hears nothing. He lives in a world of absolute silence.

It is hard to imagine a silent world but that is exactly what his world is and the world around too. There is no sound. Our planet is as silent as the others that orbit in distant skies. Your alarm clock, your laughter, the waves, the chirping birds—none make a sound. Redmond experiences a reality that most of us don't.

Any movement results in vibration, from two molecules colliding midair to the eruption of a volcano, which is a whole lot of molecules colliding at once. The vibrations are transferred to molecules in the vicinity, creating waves of vibrations. If these vibrations are strong enough to cause the ear drum to vibrate they are transferred into electrical signals which are sent to the auditory cortex in the brain where they are processed.

The brain turns those signals into what we experience as being sound. The key thing to remember is that the sound only exists in the head of the perceiver. Your experience of sound is locked within your own head. You perceive sound but it is not there. A tree growing by the side of a busy junction hears nothing of the cars and buses that rush by, it doesn't hear the pattering of the rain drops on its foliage, nor does it hear the buzz of the tree surgeon's chain saw. The tree, like Redmond exists in reality while those with functioning auditory cortices create a personal form of reality which is individual to them.

The very same principles can be applied to the other senses. The brain receives sensory information and constructs a view of the world which we assume is the same reality for everyone. There is no way of knowing. You can try to explain all you like what chocolate tastes likes or what the sunset looks like but nobody will know what your experience is like. It is personal. It is yours alone.

All creatures spend their time on Earth in solitary confinement, existing in their own reality.

Think About It

Work with a partner and try to explain to them what the ringing of a bell sounds like and the taste of chocolate. Record the types of words that each uses.

In a group take some of the words and write them on a large sheet of paper putting the most useful ones at the center of the page and the least useful toward the outer edges.

Do any of the words actually help in understanding one another's experiences?

Imagine somebody born with no senses. Make a list of what that individual might understand about the world.

The human brain only has the capacity to process five senses. If you could choose two other senses, what might you choose?

With a partner take 30 seconds each to talk about what you have learned. You should start by saying *I used to think* … and follow it up with *but now I think*…

Chapter 24

Disliking Liking

The music of the legendary Pierre Boulez was not what Ben would usually have listened to. The gentle tones of Chopin were more to his liking rather than the contemporary, avant-garde style of Boulez but when the opportunity arose to see the master conduct one of his own creations, *Notations II*, at the Berlin Philharmonie it was a chance he was happy to seize.

On arrival at the Philharmonie he negotiated his way to his seat. On the back of each seat was a piece of paper with a different seat number which informed him that the same piece was to be played twice and after the interval, seats should be swapped so the piece could be experienced from different places. He liked the novelty of the idea.

He sat and struggled with the music which seemed disjointed as if all the sounds were uncomfortable with one another. He too felt uncomfortable with them.

When the applause started to mark the end of the first half of the concert he felt relief. He had decided there was no way he could cope with listening to it for a second time and planned to leave for home at the interval.

When the lights went up the lady next to him turned to him, smiled and said, "Quite remarkable, don't you think?"

"If I'm honest it's not really my thing. I couldn't listen for a second time. I really don't like it."

"Oh, young man," she said, "It's an experience. It has nothing to do with liking. You must forget like and dislike and simply let the experience happen."

"But did you enjoy it?"

"Oh yes, I enjoyed the experience. I don't know whether I like or dislike the music. To think of it in that way is to miss the point."

He looked at her, slightly confused. "I see," he said. "So what is the point?"

She smiled at him. "Let yourself have the experience and you'll find out." With that comment swirling in his head he left the auditorium to find his pre-ordered glass of wine.

And so, after the interval he took his new seat and did as she had suggested. He didn't like the music nor did he dislike it. He felt enriched by the experience as if a door had been opened to let the sound in the way Boulez had intended.

Language is full of direct opposites: like/dislike, hard/soft, heavy/light, young/old but there are few words to fill the gaps between the two extremes. Heavy and light for example have to be qualified with words such as quite heavy, fairly light or sometimes *ish* is added as in youngish/oldish. The way language has developed suggests there is a tendency to focus on the extremes and there is not much to be interested in between. There is simply no word to describe the state between hard and soft.

In this world of polar opposites there is an assumption that everything must lie somewhere on a line between the two. Listen to a piece of music and there is an expectation that you will place it somewhere along the line between the two opposites. Anywhere from like to dislike but no matter what, a position will have to be taken.

Walk round an art gallery and viewers can be heard discussing whether they like or dislike a picture. They wrestle with their opinion and feel uncomfortable with art works which appear to jump about on the linear line partially liked, sometimes kind of liked, sometimes loved, sometimes simply not sure.

Artists and musicians often understand something different about the world and this is especially true of those who step outside the current boundaries of their art form and create something new. Often, it is not created to like or dislike but as a form of exploration of ideas. The artist and the musician create experiences. Those experiences may invoke feelings of pleasure or displeasure or even disgust but feelings are a response to the experience, not the experience per se.

Polar opposites force the individual to walk a linear line. Take a sheet of paper and draw a line across it placing the word *like* at one end and *dislike* at the other. Imagine the whole space within the paper is the range of possible experiences. Listen to a piece of music or look at a work of art. If you think in terms of like/dislike then the experience you can have is limited to the line. If the line is erased, the door is opened to an infinite possible range of responses and feelings.

Words are an integral part of daily existence. They allow the expression of a huge diverse range of emotions and feelings but they are limited. If Ben has an emotional response to something he sees or hears he is inclined to select a word which is a best fit. He also has to assume other people's understanding of the work he chooses is similar to his but he has no way of knowing whether this is actually the case.

Ben recently read a review of Chopin's Marche Funèbre which was described as being grand, stately, resolute, and then, in the trio section, by contrast, elegant, intimate, and charming. The reviewer is clearly aiming to convey an emotional response in words but it is not clear what resolute or charming music actually is. What is charming to one may not be charming to another.

There is constant pressure to describe feelings and emotions. Many social networking sites thrive on *likes* but they train the individual to think in a narrow linear fashion. Sometimes it is useful to try to translate a feeling into words but sometimes they are best just left as feelings to find their place on the sheet of paper, unlabelled.

Think About It

In a group listen to a piece of modern music. Identify different possible viewpoints for listening. It may be a person (e.g. conductor, cellist, lighting manager), a creature (e.g. a fly, a bird), or an inanimate object (e.g. a chair, the conductor's baton).

Ask each person to take a different viewpoint.

Ask each to explore how their chosen viewpoint might think of the music.

Other pupils should have the chance to ask questions to others from their viewpoint using the prompt, *I have a question to you from my viewpoint which is....*

Tell pupils to imagine all the viewpoints have vanished. Tell them they are going to listen to the piece of music again but without having a viewpoint. They can absorb the experience of the sounds but should not have a view.

Chapter 25

The Search for Life

For her ninth birthday, Annie's father, a computer systems analyst by trade, bought her a present of an AIBO dog. He'd read a lot about artificially intelligent robots and if he was honest, the present was as much to satisfy his own curiosity as it was a gift for Annie. She was an only child and with two busy working parents he was concerned that she was spending so much time alone. They often holidayed overseas and buying a real pet for her just wasn't practical. AIBO seemed like a perfect solution and wouldn't need to be taken out for walks before bedtime and wouldn't have to be house trained.

Annie loved her gift and named the robot dog, Pinkie on account of its nose. She spoke to it and would spend hours alone with it in her bedroom training it and teaching it tricks. "Clever, Pinkie," she would say stroking the length of its nose and in response it would yap in approval. She made a basket at the end of the bed and last thing at night she would read a story to Pinkie and kiss both its ears. Her parents were happy that she no longer seemed lonely, her new friend always ready to give her the attention she needed.

Six months after her birthday, Annie had been to visit her aunt in Cleveland with her parents. They drove back to New York through the night and Annie fell asleep in the back of the car clutching Pinkie to her chest. At around 2am, Pinkie appeared to wake up and let out a single distressed yap. Annie shifted in her sleep but didn't wake up. The first yap was followed by another and another. "What has set that thing off?" her father asked her mother.

"It's Pinkie. It's not a thing."

"Well what has upset Pinkie? She doesn't yap for nothing."

"Maybe she needs to be stroked."

Annie's mom stretched her arm into the back seat and gently eased the yapping dog from Annie's clutches and sat it on her lap and stroked it over its head and down the length of its back. Its tail began to wag but the yapping continued.

"I think you'll need to take the battery out. It's the only way to shut it up."

"Oh, you can't do that. It loses its memory if you take the battery out. Annie would be devastated if we did that."

"Yap, yap, yap."

"We've got another four or five hours on the road. I'm not listening to that all the way."

"I'm not removing its battery. I'm not going to be the one responsible for destroying Pinkie. Annie loves it. You know that."

"It's a robot. Just a robot. She can put the battery back in the morning and start over. Retrain it."

"But it won't be Pinkie, will it?"

"It's a robot, Jan. For goodness sake."

"It will lose all its memory."

Annie's father pulled over into a lay by. "Here, give the thing to me," he said taking Pinkie from her lap.

"You can't do it, Harry."

"Yap, yap, yap."

"Watch me," he said. He opened the battery compartment and disconnected the battery.

There was silence in the car as he passed the powerless robot back to his wife. "What are you going to tell Annie when she wakes up?"

"I'll tell her we had to stop the thing yapping and if it carries on doing it when we put the battery back in we'll get her a new one. A new Pinkie."

As the sun began to rise and the traffic on the highway slowed their journey Annie stirred from her sleep. "Where's Pinkie?" she mumbled.

"I've got him here," her mom said.

"When we have a break I'll put his battery back in. He was yapping half the night. It was the only way to stop him."

"Daddy, you didn't take his battery out?"

"He'll be fine once it's back in."

Annie burst into tears and cried, "You killed him, Daddy. You killed Pinkie."

"He'll be all better once we put the battery back in," her mom said.

"But he'll have forgotten everything. You've killed him. He's dead."

"Annie, dear, he's only a robot. He was never really alive."

"Yes he was. He was my pet and you've killed him."

Annie was convinced her robot was more than an artificial intelligence toy. For her, it was alive in the same way her parents were. It had a set of personal memories and it had learned things she had taught it in the same way her parents had taught her. For Annie, this emotional bond and shared history was enough for it to be considered to be alive. Pinkie had engaged with her emotions and her upset over its demise had a real impact on her. For her father, who didn't have an emotional relationship with the toy, it was no more than an ingenious piece of software programming, housed in a shell made from manufactured components, and was no more alive than his programmable watch.

The distinction between alive and not alive at first seems like a very simple one. It appears simple to agree that a mouse is alive and a rock is not. The mouse has a nervous system and is capable of independent action, it breathes, and has a beating heart. The rock is lacking in all of these attributes. A tree, however, lacks those attributes too but most would consider it be alive. The robot has internal circuitry which in some respects is similar to the nervous system of an animal in that it relies on electric impulses and to some extent it reacts according to external stimuli. Annie had trained its electrical impulses to perform certain acts and the robotic dog reacted to stimuli in the same way a mouse might but like the tree, the robot does not breath nor does it have a beating heart.

Science attempts to break down the human body or the mouse's body or a bacterium or sunflower into component parts that are all understandable in scientific terms. Each can be said to be a machine. Perhaps scientists are only beginning to understand the workings of the human brain and it may be that a full understanding is beyond the scope of human intelligence but it is considered a machine nevertheless with the potential for understanding. Annie's robotic dog is also a machine albeit a far simpler one. What is the difference?

It might be expected that biology is the best place to look for a concrete, scientific answer to the difference between being alive and not alive. The two most commonly distinguishing features of life are the ability to grow and the ability to reproduce but there are situations which don't fit comfortably.

In nature, there are examples of bacteria which enter very long dormant periods when they do not grow nor metabolize in any way but they are still considered to be alive. A fire can be said to grow and consume energy but is not considered to be alive. The *turritopsis nutricula*, is a type of jellyfish which is immortal, being able to alternate between adult and juvenile stages; in a sense it both grows and shrinks indefinitely but is clearly alive. Consider the petal of a plant. When attached to the plant it is considered to have life and when dried and lying on the ground it has no life. The second the petal falls from the plant the cells have not ceased to work; thus, it is hard to agree at what precise point the petal changed from being alive to being not alive. Growth on its own cannot give us a satisfactory definition of life.

Turning to reproduction it is true to say that a male and a female dog can reproduce but a single dog on its own is not capable of reproduction, nor is an animal which has been neutered and yet both are very much alive. The robot may not be able to reproduce in the conventional sense but it is, in theory, possible to program a robot to build another robot thereby creating future species of the same robot. Furthermore, flaws in the building process may eventually lead to new species of robots in much the same way as the conventional process of evolution does.

Neither growth, nor reproduction as definition can rule out the possibility that the robotic dog is in fact alive.

As yet, the scientific community has not been able to arrive at an agreed definition of what life actually is and what appeared at first to be a simple and rather obvious question turns out to be baffling for even the greatest of minds.

Many people are uncomfortable with the idea of robots being considered to be alive and agree there is something missing from the robot but nobody is quite sure what that missing element is.

The robotic dog and a real dog are both machines. One is biological, the other not but that doesn't seem sufficient evidence to say one is alive and the other is not. To complicate matters further, the future of computing may lie in biocomputing where DNA and proteins are the working components. What's more, these biocomputers will have the capacity to self-assemble, regenerate, and replicate themselves. Whether they have life is another matter entirely.

Think About It

Work in groups of three or four.

Your task is to make a claim about robotic animals in terms of the having life or not and think how your group can support the claim. Then think of a question you predict the others in the class might ask.

Each group should present their claim and support to the class. Once presented other groups can have the opportunity to ask a question. It is not necessary for the questions to answered. The power of the thinking is in the questioning.

On a post-it note write one thing that is crucial in defining something as being alive.

Chapter 26

Confusion

Paulina is an enthusiastic young computer animator. She is only thirteen but her work has won accolades and her animations have six-figure viewings on YouTube. Her father is impressed with her talents and encourages them by buying her up-to-date computers which can cope with memory-sapping graphics and he invests in the latest software to help Paulina master her craft.

Her mother, while proud of her daughter's achievements is concerned that she spends too much time on her computer and seems to be neglecting healthy friendships.

She spoke to Paulina about her concerns and said, "It's great what you do but it's important to do everything in moderation."

Paulina thought for a moment and said, "Then that means I must also be moderate about doing things in moderation. So sometimes I don't need to be moderate."

Her mother looked confused and told Paulina not to be cheeky claiming she knew perfectly well what she meant.

She did, but she chose to use her logic to decode her mother's language precisely. Her mother's message was obvious. Her intention was understood but her language was inaccurate and didn't convey the message clearly.

In a world of fast language where emails, texts, and instant messages are the common currency of communication, attention to meaning and detail are too often neglected. Effective communication does not translate into more or faster communication. To be effective, language must be used carefully lest the message be misunderstood, misinterpreted or, at worst, confused and illogical and just meaningless. Careless language leaves the perpetrator vulnerable to attack as anyone in political life knows well.

A long time ago, philosophers realized that their grand theories would be scrutinized very closely. The philosopher is free to make any claim he or she wants but illogical or unclear thinking will be exposed and with it a theory along with one's personal credibility will tumble. For this reason, philosophers always aim to express themselves with great clarity. Although fast communication has become the norm there is much power to be gleaned from carefully composed language.

The most common errors are as follows:

FUZZY CONCEPTS

Many people in this day and age will justify an action or choice of purchase on the grounds that *it is cool*. When one asks what is actually meant by the word *cool* there is usually a look of incredulity on the face of the utterer. The speaker, typically, has a vague idea of what he/she meant but either they are too lazy to express their idea clearly or they are unable or unwilling to define what is a very fuzzy concept. *Cool* is so fuzzy has virtually no meaning even though it is so commonly used.
Language is full of these ill-defined concepts.

Rome is beautiful.
Golden Labradors are nice.

Neither give the listener any meaningful information because one person's idea of *nice* or *beautiful* can be very different to another's.

Many so-called fuzzy concepts involve matters of degree. There is no accepted norm and, as a result, the concepts are vague in their meaning. Consider the following:

He is thin.
Her father is intelligent.
It is cold today.

The terms *cold*, *intelligent*, and *thin* are all relative. Thus, what is cold to an Alaskan citizen will be different to the cold of a Texan. Misunderstandings arise from the fact that there is no universally agreed norm that the concepts are relative to.

THE IMPOSSIBLE QUESTION

When did you stop biting your nails?

This seems to be a straightforward question. If the answer is *I didn't*, there are two possible meanings. If you never bit your nails in the first place it would be true to say you did not stop. One cannot stop something one never started. If you did bite your nails in the past then the answer suggests you are still biting them. The problem lies in the careless question. The questioner was seeking information but the structure of the question means the reply cannot supply them with an accurate answer.

Sometimes a question is impossible to answer.

Why did you do that?

Nobody can ever fully understand why they did anything so to answer the question it is necessary to think in terms of what sort of answer will satisfy the questioner but this may be very far from the truth.

CIRCULAR ARGUMENTS

Everything I tell you is a lie.

This is a classic example of a circular reference. The meaning appears to be clear until it is considered more carefully. If the statement is true, then it follows that the statement must also be a lie. If the statement is a lie, then it follows that everything I tell you is true which means everything I tell you is a lie. The argument goes round in circles and makes no sense. Such arguments are surprisingly common and the astute thinker will become aware of them.

It is often stated that money is the root of all evil because money lies at the heart of all human misery. Close analysis reveals the illogical nature of the argument and can be expressed in a simple form.

A causes B because B is caused by A

Expressed in this way it is obvious that there is no actual argument.

Illogical Conclusions

New Yorkers are open minded.
Open minded people are successful.
New Yorkers are successful.

The problem here is that New Yorkers are not referred to in the second statement or premise. The conclusion that New Yorkers are successful is an over generalization. It might be true but that conclusion cannot be drawn from the information given even though it may seem plausible.

All cats have four legs.
Cats are mammals.
All mammals have four legs.

This example follows the same principle of over generalization as the first but is more obviously ridiculous in its conclusion.

The astute thinker will always be on guard and will be able to detect the same principle in more complex arguments.

USE OF STATISTICS

Statistics are often quoted in to support arguments but they are often used inappropriately. This can be accidental but is often deliberate in an attempt to influence opinion. The philosophical thinker should slow down when statistics are used, consider them carefully before deciding whether they give support to an argument or whether they are a sign of weakness.

Consider the following:

Women are safer drivers than men. 75% of all accidents are caused by male drivers.

The second statement may be true but the conclusion cannot be taken from this information. It is necessary to know what percentage of total drivers are women.

Over the last 20 years overall life expectancy in the USA has gone up to 76 for males and 81 for females. It is clear that people in the USA are living healthier lives than they used to.

This seems like a plausible conclusion but it over simplifies the situation and ignores the possibility of other factors, e.g. better medicines, the availability of medicines, better health care for the elderly, higher standards of living conditions.

Statistics only have meaning when they are gathered for large sample populations and they do not apply to an individual sample of one.

It may be true to say that *76% of smokers die from smoking related illnesses* but when you consider an individual smoker there is no way of knowing whether they will lie in the 76% who will suffer from a smoking related illness or whether they will lie in the 24% who don't. The general statistic does not inform us about an individual.

A hotel chain claims: *Only 3% of our customers complain. We have a 97% satisfaction rate.*

This assumes there are only two alternatives. It is like saying if it is not black, it must be white. The shades of gray have been conveniently ignored. It is wrong to draw the conclusion that a customer was satisfied simply because they didn't complain.

Throughout life, decisions have to be made. Some may involve personal arguments that never need to leave the individual's own head, some require thorough debating as in politics, some require evaluating the input from other team members as in the commercial world, some demand an evaluation of research papers and a careful consideration of conclusions as seen in the scientific world.

Good decisions are always logical decisions but to ensure logic both time and care are needed least one fall prey to some of the errors of thought outlined above. In a world that demands fast-moving, virtually instant communication there is a greater need than ever to be aware of and alert to illogical reasoning.

Think About It

A paradox is something which appears to make complete sense but the conclusion is clearly nonsensical.

Read the following paradox:

One Friday afternoon a maths teacher announces to his class that he will give them a surprise test the following week.

"You can't," Ben said.

"Yes I can. I'm going to," the teacher said.

"No, I mean you can't, as in, it's impossible."

"How do work that one out?"

"Well, you can't give it to us on Friday because if we didn't get it Monday, Tuesday, Wednesday or Thursday then we would know it would have to be on Friday so it wouldn't be a surprise."

"True," the teacher said looking confused.

Ben continued. "And it can't be on Thursday because if we didn't get it Monday, Tuesday, Wednesday then we would know it would have to be on Thursday so it wouldn't be a surprise. And it can't be on Wednesday because if we didn't get it Monday or Tuesday then we would know it would to be on Wednesday so it wouldn't be a surprise.

And it can't be on Tuesday because if we didn't get it on Monday then we would know it would to be on Tuesday so it wouldn't be a surprise.

That only leaves Monday but that's the only day it could be so it wouldn't be a surprise either. So, you see, it's impossible."

Work in a small group and discuss the paradox. Make a claim that Ben is correct in his reasoning or incorrect.

Think how you can support your claim.

What question would your group ask to help clarify the situation?

Chapter 27

Waking Dreams

Jack Teller spent a total of 38 years in an asylum in New England until his death at the age of 69. On leaving college, he'd travelled round India dipping his mind into Hindu and Buddhist philosophies, meditating and writing a volume of poetry. He became absorbed in the spiritual dimensions of his life and when he returned to his New England home in Canton Valley he struggled to adjust. He took jobs in gas stations and factories until he secured a job as an archivist in Hartford Public library.

Life among books and papers made Jack feel enclosed and believing he was a reincarnation of the Hindu deity, Varuna, god of water, he made his way to Hotchkiss Cove where he stole a boat and rowed out to Horse Island. Here, he kept guard over Long Island Sound, saying prayers for every boat that passed. He lived on the tiny island, completely naked for over a year until he was discovered by a police patrol.

He had protested at being removed from the island but, concerned for his welfare, he was taken to Yale-New Haven hospital for psychiatric assessment and the subsequent diagnosis saw Jack confined to a psychiatric hospital where he lived permanently until his death in 1983.

Every night Jack had kept a diary. There were many volumes and after his death they were passed to his only surviving relative, an aunt whom he'd never met. To her surprise every single entry of every volume was identical.

When I go to sleep the first thing I do is look out of the window. I sit at the small wooden table in the room and run my fingertips over the deep scratches. Outside, there is a garden and a large oak tree. There is a bench under the branches by the trunk and sometimes people who appear to be patients sit there and stare. Most days the dream is the same. I write a little sitting at the wooden table by the window then someone who appears as a nurse tells me to dress and wash.

There is a hall with perhaps twenty long wooden tables and I am taken there to eat then I am led to a chair. It's old and stained. It is a deep red color and has wings that protect my ears. Sometimes when I sit there the dream ends and I wake up.

When I'm awake, different things happen, people aren't stuck with the one face. They can be one person one minute and then another the next minute or sometimes they can merge. And I can move through spaces without tiring. Sometimes I can fly over the hospital and over whole cities or I can take giant leaps over the trees. The world is rich and full of colors and excitement but then I fall asleep again and every time it is the same dream. The same nurse, the same chair and tables.

I never like sleeping. I try to stay awake as much as I can but there is an awful bell which sounds every day. I never like it because it sends me to sleep and if I ignore it a nurse shakes me until I fall into monotonous slumber.

His aunt was confused when she read this diary entry but one of the nurses did indeed confirm that he claimed he was dreaming when he was awake and when he fell asleep he believed he woke up in his real world.

At first this seems bizarre but could it be that Jack was right? Everything that appears real is created within the individual's head. There is sensory input and the brain takes the information and turns it into a sense of reality. It is a personal reality and there is no way of knowing that this is the same reality shared by others. There is an assumption that what person A experiences as reality is the same as what person B experiences. But is it right to make this assumption?

Imagine 100 people sitting in a room and each has a box in front of them. The first person opens their box and there is a beetle in it. There is no logical reason to assume every other box will also contain a beetle. It follows that it is not logical to assume the reality in one person's head is the same reality that occupies the other 99 people's heads but this is precisely the assumption most people make.

So, sensory input leads to an experience of reality but it also stimulates thoughts. You can sit there and wander around your bedroom in your head or you can imagine yourself crunching an apple. These imaginary experiences are also creations of the brain but for some reason they are not considered to be real. Most would regard the thoughts themselves as being real but not the content those thoughts generate although both exist in the form of neural activity in the brain. It is not clear why one form of brain activity is considered to be imaginary whilst the other is elevated to the status of reality.

When Jack was dreaming, the images and experiences in his brain appeared real. Just as in waking life, the brain works with the information it has to create, images, sounds, tastes, and smells and so in sleep it uses that same information to create a reality. Events in dreams elicit biological responses such as increased heart rate, the production of sweat, and the release of hormones so, in this sense, his dream experiences have a real effect on the body.

In his dreams, his actions appeared to have an effect on others and he had control over his actions or at least, he had the feeling of control. In waking life, he had a similar feeling of control but this may have been as real or as illusionary as the control experienced in dreams.

The interactions a person has on a daily basis shape and influence the development of the personality. Perhaps the same can be said of dreams. Feelings of guilt or anger in a dream may indeed have a role to play in the ongoing construct which is personality. Science will never find an answer to this but that doesn't stop it from being a possibility.

It may well be that what happens in the waking world and the sleeping world and the thoughts that circulate between are all part of the same reality or all part of the same illusion.

Think About It

Read Jack's diary entry again.

How does anything you has read connect with what you understand about the world?

In what ways have your thinking been extended or challenged by Jack's view of the world?

What aspects of his diary do you find have challenged your way of thinking? What issues would you like to explore more?

Share your ideas with a group or class.

About the Author

Ron Gilmore completed his master's degree in psychology before entering the teaching profession. He has 25 years of experience working as an educator in schools in Asia and Europe and has used philosophy in many aspects of his classroom practise. He currently lives and works in Berlin.

www.ingramcontent.com/pod-product-compliance
Lightning Source LLC
Chambersburg PA
CBHW021304240426
43669CB00041B/139